SONY AND EPSILON: LESSONS FOR DATA SECURITY LEGISLATION

HEARING

BEFORE THE

SUBCOMMITTEE ON COMMERCE, MANUFACTURING, AND TRADE

OF THE

COMMITTEE ON ENERGY AND COMMERCE

HOUSE OF REPRESENTATIVES

ONE HUNDRED TWELFTH CONGRESS

FIRST SESSION

JUNE 2, 2011

Serial No. 112–55

Printed for the use of the Committee on Energy and Commerce

energycommerce.house.gov

U.S. GOVERNMENT PRINTING OFFICE

71–258 PDF   WASHINGTON : 2012

For sale by the Superintendent of Documents, U.S. Government Printing Office
Internet: bookstore.gpo.gov   Phone: toll free (866) 512–1800; DC area (202) 512–1800
Fax: (202) 512–2104   Mail: Stop IDCC, Washington, DC 20402–0001

COMMITTEE ON ENERGY AND COMMERCE

FRED UPTON, Michigan
Chairman

JOE BARTON, Texas
  Chairman Emeritus
CLIFF STEARNS, Florida
ED WHITFIELD, Kentucky
JOHN SHIMKUS, Illinois
JOSEPH R. PITTS, Pennsylvania
MARY BONO MACK, California
GREG WALDEN, Oregon
LEE TERRY, Nebraska
MIKE ROGERS, Michigan
SUE WILKINS MYRICK, North Carolina
  Vice Chairman
JOHN SULLIVAN, Oklahoma
TIM MURPHY, Pennsylvania
MICHAEL C. BURGESS, Texas
MARSHA BLACKBURN, Tennessee
BRIAN P. BILBRAY, California
CHARLES F. BASS, New Hampshire
PHIL GINGREY, Georgia
STEVE SCALISE, Louisiana
ROBERT E. LATTA, Ohio
CATHY McMORRIS RODGERS, Washington
GREGG HARPER, Mississippi
LEONARD LANCE, New Jersey
BILL CASSIDY, Louisiana
BRETT GUTHRIE, Kentucky
PETE OLSON, Texas
DAVID B. McKINLEY, West Virginia
CORY GARDNER, Colorado
MIKE POMPEO, Kansas
ADAM KINZINGER, Illinois
H. MORGAN GRIFFITH, Virginia

HENRY A. WAXMAN, California
  Ranking Member
JOHN D. DINGELL, Michigan
EDWARD J. MARKEY, Massachusetts
EDOLPHUS TOWNS, New York
FRANK PALLONE, JR., New Jersey
BOBBY L. RUSH, Illinois
ANNA G. ESHOO, California
ELIOT L. ENGEL, New York
GENE GREEN, Texas
DIANA DeGETTE, Colorado
LOIS CAPPS, California
MICHAEL F. DOYLE, Pennsylvania
JANICE D. SCHAKOWSKY, Illinois
CHARLES A. GONZALEZ, Texas
JAY INSLEE, Washington
TAMMY BALDWIN, Wisconsin
MIKE ROSS, Arkansas
ANTHONY D. WEINER, New York
JIM MATHESON, Utah
G.K. BUTTERFIELD, North Carolina
JOHN BARROW, Georgia
DORIS O. MATSUI, California
DONNA M. CHRISTENSEN, Virgin Islands

(II)

CONTENTS

SONY AND EPSILON: LESSONS FOR DATA SECURITY LEGISLATION

THURSDAY, JUNE 2, 2011

House of Representatives,
Subcommittee on Commerce, Manufacturing, and
Trade,
Committee on Energy and Commerce,
Washington, DC.

The subcommittee met, pursuant to call, at 12:05 p.m., in room 2123 of the Rayburn House Office Building, Hon. Mary Bono Mack (chairwoman of the subcommittee) presiding.

Members present: Representatives Bono Mack, Blackburn, Stearns, Harper, Lance, Guthrie, Olson, McKinley, Pompeo, Kinzinger, and Butterfield.

Staff present: Charlotte Baker, Press Secretary; Allison Busbee, Legislative Clerk; Paul Cancienne, Policy Coordinator, Commerce, Manufacturing and Trade; Brian McCullough, Senior Professional Staff Member, Commerce, Manufacturing and Trade; Gib Mullan, Chief Counsel, Commerce, Manufacturing and Trade; Shannon Weinberg, Counsel, Commerce, Manufacturing and Trade; Michelle Ash, Democratic Chief Counsel; Felipe Mendoza, Democratic Counsel; and Will Wallace, Democratic Policy Analyst.

OPENING STATEMENT OF HON. MARY BONO MACK, A REPRESENTATIVE IN CONGRESS FROM THE STATE OF CALIFORNIA

Mrs. Bono Mack. Good afternoon. If the room would please come to order. Guests, kindly take your seats. Thank you. So good afternoon.

In today's online world, your name, birth date, and mother's maiden name are often used to verify your identity. But in the wake of massive data breaches at Sony and Epsilon, we are now painfully more aware that this very same information can be used just as easily to falsify your identity. The time has come for Congress to take action. And the chair now recognizes herself for an opening statement.

With nearly 1.5 billion credit cards now in use in the United States and more and more Americans banking and shopping online, cyber thieves have a treasure chest of opportunities today to get rich quick. Why crack a vault when you can hack a network? The Federal Trade Commission estimates that nearly 9 million Americans fall victim to identity theft every year, costing consumers and businesses billions of dollars annually, and those numbers are growing steadily and alarmingly.

In recent years, sophisticated and carefully orchestrated cyber attacks designed to obtain personal information about consumers, especially when it comes to their credit cards, have become one of the fastest-growing criminal enterprises here in the U.S., as well as across the world. Just last month, the Justice Department shut down a cyber crime ring believed to be based in Russia, which was responsible for the online theft of up to $100 million.

The boldness of these attacks and the threat they present to unsuspecting Americans was underscored recently by massive data breaches at Epsilon and Sony. In some ways, Sony has become Ground Zero in the war to protect consumers' online information. The initial attacks on Sony's PlayStation network and online entertainment services, which put some 100 million customer accounts at risk, were quickly followed by still more attacks at other Sony divisions and subsidiaries. Since then, the company, to its credit, has taken some very aggressive steps to prevent future cyber attacks such as installing new firewalls, enhancing data protection, and enhancing their encryption capabilities, expanding automated software monitoring, and hiring a new chief information security officer.

These are all important new safeguards, but with millions of American consumers in harm's way, why weren't these safety protocols already in place? For me, one of the most troubling issues is how long it took Sony to notify consumers and the way in which the company did it—by posting an announcement on its blog. In effect, Sony put the burden on consumers to search for information instead of providing it to them directly. That cannot happen again.

While I remain critical of Sony's initial handling of these data breaches, as well as its decision not to testify at our last hearing—and that goes for Epsilon as well—it is clear that since then, the company has been systematically targeted by hackers and cyber thieves who are constantly probing Sony's security systems for weaknesses and opportunities to infiltrate its networks.

So today, I am not here to point fingers. Instead, let us point the way, a better, smarter way to protect American consumers online. As I have said, you shouldn't have to cross your fingers and whisper a prayer whenever you type in a credit card number on your computer and hit ''Enter.'' E-commerce is a vital and growing part of our economy. We should take steps to embrace and protect it and that starts with robust cyber security.

As chairman of the subcommittee, I believe the lessons learned from the Sony and Epsilon experiences can be instructive. How did these breaches occur? What steps are being taken to prevent future breaches? What is being done to mitigate the effects of these breaches? And what policies should be in place to better protect American consumers in the future. Most importantly, consumers have a right to know when their personal information has been compromised, and companies have an overriding responsibility to promptly alert them. These recent data breaches only reinforce my long-held belief that much more needs to be done to protect sensitive consumer information.

Americans need additional safeguards to prevent identity theft, and I will soon introduce legislation designed to accomplish this goal. My legislation will be crafted around 3 guiding principles.

First, companies and entities that hold personal information must establish and maintain security policies to prevent the unauthorized acquisition of that data. Second, information considered especially sensitive such as credit card numbers should have even more robust security safeguards in place. And finally, consumers should be promptly informed when their personal information has been jeopardized.

The time has come for Congress to take decisive action. We need a uniformed national standard for data security and data breach notification and we need it now. While I remain hopeful that law enforcement officials will quickly determine the extent of these latest cyber attacks, they serve as a reminder that all companies have a responsibility to protect personal information and to promptly notify consumers when that information has been put at risk. And we have a responsibility as lawmakers to make certain that this happens.

[The prepared statement of Mrs. Bono Mack follows:]

PREPARED STATEMENT OF HON. MARY BONO MACK

With nearly 1.5 billion credit cards now in use in the United States—and more and more Americans banking and shopping online—cyber thieves have a treasure chest of opportunities today to ''get rich quick.'' Why crack a vault when you can hack a network?

The Federal Trade Commission estimates that nearly nine million Americans fall victim to identity theft every year, costing consumers and businesses billions of dollars annually—and those numbers are growing steadily and alarmingly.

In recent years, sophisticated and carefully orchestrated cyber attacks—designed to obtain personal information about consumers, especially when it comes to their credit cards—have become one of the fastest growing criminal enterprises here in the United States and across the world.

Just last month, the Justice Department shut down a cyber crime ring—believed to be based in Russia -which was responsible for the online theft of up to $100 million. The boldness of these attacks and the threat they present to unsuspecting Americans was underscored recently by massive data breaches at Epsilon and Sony.

In some ways, Sony has become ground zero in the war to protect consumers' online information. The initial attacks on Sony's PlayStation Network and online entertainment services—which put some 100 million customer accounts at risk—were quickly followed by still more attacks at other Sony divisions and subsidiaries.

Since then, the company—to its credit—has taken some very aggressive steps to prevent future cyber attacks, such as installing new firewalls.enhancing data protection and encryption capabilities. expanding automated software monitoring.and hiring a new Chief Information Security Officer.

These are all important new safeguards, but with millions of American consumers in harm's way, why weren't these safety protocols already in place?

For me, one of the most troubling issues is how long it took Sony to notify consumers.and the way in which the company did it—by posting an announcement on its blog. In effect, Sony put the burden on consumers to search for information instead of providing it to them directly. That cannot happen again.

While I remain critical of Sony's initial handling of these data breaches—as well as its decision not to testify at our last hearing.and that goes for Epsilon as well—it's clear that since then the company has been systematically targeted by hackers and cyber thieves who are constantlyprobing Sony's security systems for weaknesses and opportunities to infiltrate its networks.

So today, let's not point fingers. Instead, let's point the way—a better, smarter way—to protect American consumers online. As I have said, you shouldn't have to cross your fingers and whisper a prayer when you type in a credit card number on your computer and hit ''enter.'' E-commerce is a vital and growing part of our economy. We should take steps to embrace and protect it—and that starts with robust cyber security.

As Chairman of this Subcommittee, I believe the lessons learned from the Sony and Epsilon experiences can be instructive. How did these breaches occur? What steps are being taken to prevent future breaches? What's being done to mitigate the effects of these breaches? And what policies should be in place to better protect American consumers in the future?

Most importantly, consumers have a right to know when their personal information has been compromised, and companies have an overriding responsibility to promptly alert them.

These recent data breaches only reinforce my long-held belief that much more needs to be done to protect sensitive consumer information. Americans need additional safeguards to prevent identity theft, and I will soon introduce legislation designed to accomplish this goal. My legislation will be crafted around three guiding principles:

First, companies and entities that hold personal information must establish and maintain security policies to prevent the unauthorized acquisition of that data;

Second, information considered especially sensitive, such as credit card numbers, should have even more robust security safeguards;

And finally, consumers should be promptly informed when their personal information has been jeopardized.

The time has come for Congress to take decisive action. We need a uniform national standard for data security and data breach notification, and we need it now.

While I remain hopeful that law enforcement officials will quickly determine the extent of these latest cyber attacks, they serves as a reminder that all companies have a responsibility to protect personal information and to promptly notify consumers when that information has been put at risk. And we have a responsibility, as lawmakers, to make certain this happens.

Mrs. BONO MACK. And now I would like to recognize the vice chairman of the—oh, I am sorry—the ranking member Mr. Butterfield for his 5-minute opening statement.

OPENING STATEMENT OF HON. G.K. BUTTERFIELD, A REPRESENTATIVE IN CONGRESS FROM THE STATE OF NORTH CAROLINA

Mr. BUTTERFIELD. Let me thank you, Chairman Bono Mack, for your indulgence. I have been in my office with 28 constituents, one of whom was a World War II veteran and several Vietnam veterans and they wanted to take pictures and you know that drill. And so I had to accommodate them as best I could. But we are here and thank you very much for convening this hearing today. And I certainly thank the two witnesses for your presence.

Madam Chairman, thank you for holding this hearing on data security and the recent breaches that we have seen at Sony and Epsilon. Last month, well over 100 million consumer records have been compromised as a result of those breaches, including full names, email and mailing addresses, the passwords, and maybe even credit card numbers. Those two major breaches illustrate that no company is safe from attack and that we must always operate at a heightened level of security and vigilance. No company wants its data compromised, and Sony and Epsilon are certainly no exception.

Sony was victim to hackers who stole nearly 100 million consumer records, and it took engineers several days to realize that there was an intrusion. During that time, hackers had full access to Sony's servers. The breach that occurred at Epsilon was very large and involved the names and email addresses of about 50 of Epsilon's clients with conservative estimates of 60 million records stolen. Luckily, no critically sensitive information was stolen, but it easily could have.

It is important that businesses do all they can do to protect consumers from having their information fall into the wrong hands. For many Americans, shopping, paying bills, and refilling prescriptions and communicating with friends and family and even playing games are all done online. As people share more and more information online, the potential for personally identifiable information to be compromised increases exponentially. Names, physical addresses, dates of birth, Social Security numbers, and credit card numbers are just a few of the types of information that hackers are able to access and exploit.

While 46 States have laws requiring consumer notification when a breach occurs, there is currently no federal standard to address this. Moreover, there is no federal law requiring companies that hold PII to have reasonable safeguards in place to protect this information. Without a federal standard, I am concerned that American consumers remain largely exposed online. And during the 109th Congress and subsequent Congresses, members of this committee worked in a bipartisan fashion to develop the Data, Accountability, and Trust Act to address the issue of data security.

The DATA bill of the 111th Congress by my friend and former chairman of the subcommittee Mr. Rush from Illinois would have required entities holding data containing personal information to adopt reasonable and appropriate security measures to safeguard it and, in the event of a breach, to notify affected individuals. The DATA bill passed the House and the 111th Congress but our friends in the Senate did not act. The DATA bill is a good foundation to improve the security of e-commerce, something that is good for consumers and good for business. It would give American consumers more peace of mind about online transactions and make them more likely to continue and expand their use of online services.

And so, Madam Chairman, we have learned a lot from the breaches at Sony and Epsilon and I expect to learn more today from our two witnesses. I want you to know that I stand ready to work with you and our colleagues to pass a strong bipartisan data security bill like the DATA bill that we saw in the last session. I thank today's witnesses for their testimony and look forward to each of you. Thank you very much. I yield back.

Mrs. BONO MACK. I thank the gentleman. Chairman Upton yielded his 5 minutes for an opening statement to me in accordance with committee rules. And as his designee, I now recognize Mrs. Blackburn for 2 minutes.

OPENING STATEMENT OF HON. MARSHA BLACKBURN, A REPRESENTATIVE IN CONGRESS FROM THE STATE OF TENNESSEE

Mrs. BLACKBURN. Thank you, Madam Chairman. I will submit my full statement.

A couple of comments. I think that the Sony and the Epsilon breaches raise a lot of questions with our constituents. What they are asking us is, number one, how do you minimize identity theft? Number two, they want proper notifications from the venders that they are doing business with. And number three, they want to see better coordination with law enforcement. They feel as if this is missing. And I know that as we address this, what we are going to have to look at is better government coordination, incentives for industry cooperation in this issue, stricter penalty deterrents against hackers, and a flexible framework for risk assessment and breach alerts.

As we do this, I hope that we will continue to look at the threat of digital protection of intellectual property. The two are inter-related and they both deserve attention. And I have to tell you, with the new music cloud services from Apple, Google, and Amazon, my concern is there that we hold everybody accountable and secure the integrity of that system.

I do want to highlight that on the issue of the illegal downloads and file sharing, my home State of Tennessee has just passed and signed into law a bill that puts in place penalties for this. They have made this a crime in our State, and I am glad they did it because losing content to the rogue Web sites not only becomes an issue for the entertainment industry, but it exposes consumers to viruses, dangerous products, and increases the likelihood of data theft.

So I thank you all for being here and I yield back my time.

[The prepared statement of Mrs. Blackburn follows:]

Prepared Statement of Hon. Marsha Blackburn

I thank the Chair for holding this hearing on securing our online data and privacy.

This is a timely subject of importance not only for our economy, but also for our virtual and physical safety.

Last year Tennessee ranked 18th for fraud, and 19th for identity theft complaints nationwide. But the disturbing proliferation of data theft knows no boundaries in the virtual marketplace. And the Epsilon and the two Sony breaches raise the stakes of our policy response.

Just this week, after problems with the Android app for Skype were apparently fixed, consumers reported receiving robo-calls soliciting their credit card information.

Representatives from the industry have an obligation to explain to the American people exactly how our data is being hijacked, and what exactly they plan to do about it.

In examining the lifecycle of these data breaches, an obvious and disturbing pattern can been seen in lagging consumer notifications. It's a trend I fear perpetuates industry's ''culture of damage control''—a business strategy that accelerates identity theft and virtual phishing schemes.

We need a framework that gives consumers at least a fighting chance to protect the ''Virtual You''—one's online identity—not just the false sense of security they have been fed.

I look forward to the witnesses' testimony, and to an open discussion about how we can secure our data and privacy in the virtual realm. I yield my time.

Mrs. Bono Mack. I thank the gentlelady. And the chair recognizes Mr. Stearns for 2 minutes.

OPENING STATEMENT OF HON. CLIFF STEARNS, A REPRESENTATIVE IN CONGRESS FROM THE STATE OF FLORIDA

Mr. Stearns. Thank you, Madam Chair.

I think it is mentioned by the chairwoman, the FTC recently reported 9 million Americans have fallen victim to identity theft. And I think it is sort of puzzling, a corporation as strong and comprehensive as Sony, they would, you would think, have the ability to certify that their data is secure. As recently mentioned, over 45 States have adopted a data breach notification requirement, but, of course, there is no law on a federal basis. So it is good that you folks are here so we can ask you some questions about, you know, perhaps if you know who the people were, what was the requirements that you set up in a corporation as extensive as Sony, and do you think there is a criminal case here that should be prosecuted? So there are lots of questions so I appreciate your coming here.

As many of you know, I had a bill when I was chairman of the subcommittee that we got out of the House. Unfortunately, it did not get through the Senate. And I have introduced it with Mr. Matheson again, which simply required the Federal Trade Commission to develop these regulations requiring persons that own or possess electronic data to establish necessary security policies and procedures, as well as notification mechanism.

So both of our witnesses today certainly have within their power to provide the software, the data security provisions that are necessary. I think it must be puzzling to them as well as to us why this happened to them considering how sophisticated both of them are. I have had the opportunity to talk to them in my office, so it is very appreciative that you took the time to come here and talk to us and we look forward to your testimony. Thank you.

Mrs. BONO MACK. I thank the gentleman. And the chair recognizes Mr. Olson for 1 minute.

OPENING STATEMENT OF HON. PETE OLSON, A REPRESENTATIVE IN CONGRESS FROM THE STATE OF TEXAS

Mr. OLSON. I thank the chairwoman for her leadership in calling this timely hearing.

As we all learned this morning, overseas hackers from China hacked into Google email accounts. Like Sony, Epsilon, and now Google, my home State of Texas has experienced a massive data breach in April of this year when almost 3.5 million Texans had their personal information, their names, mailing addresses, and Social Security numbers compromised from the office of the Texas Comptroller of Public Accounts, and it was posted to a public server.

There is a clear need for government, businesses, and citizens to work together to protect citizens' personal information. I look forward to working with the chairwoman on comprehensive data security legislation.

I thank the witnesses for coming. I yield back the balance of my time.

Mrs. BONO MACK. I thank the gentleman and turn our attention to the panel. We have a single panel of very distinguished witnesses joining us today. Welcome. Each of you have a prepared statement that will be placed into the record, but if you could summarize your statements in your remarks, we would appreciate it.

On our panel, we have Jeanette Fitzgerald, General Counsel for Epsilon Data Management, LLC. Also testifying is Tim Schaaff, President, Sony Network Entertainment International. Good afternoon, and thank you both very much for coming. You will each be recognized, as I said, for 5 minutes. To help you keep track of time, there is a clever little device in front of you: red, yellow, green. And when the light turns yellow, please summarize as you would a traffic light.

So Ms. Fitzgerald, you are recognized for 5 minutes. And please remember the microphone and pull it close to your mouth if you would.

STATEMENTS OF JEANETTE FITZGERALD, GENERAL COUNSEL, EPSILON DATA MANAGEMENT, LLC; AND TIM SCHAAFF, PRESIDENT, SONY NETWORK ENTERTAINMENT INTERNATIONAL

STATEMENT OF JEANETTE FITZGERALD

Ms. FITZGERALD. Ranking Member Butterfield, and distinguished members of——

Mrs. BONO MACK. Sorry. Excuse me. Would you pull the microphone up?

Ms. FITZGERALD. Closer? Better?

Mrs. BONO MACK. Thank you.

Ms. FITZGERALD. Good morning. Chairman Bono Mack, Ranking Member Butterfield, and distinguished members of the subcommittee, my name is Jeanette Fitzgerald, and I am the general counsel for Epsilon Data Management. Thank you for inviting me to present Epsilon's testimony on data security. I hope that I can provide information today in going forward that will act as a helpful resource as you consider data security legislation that is in the best interest of both consumers and business. My full written testimony has been submitted for the record. I will summarize it here and hope to leave you with three main points.

First, who is Epsilon and how do we provide important data management services for our clients? Second, how the attack of March 30 occurred and what we are doing to apprehend the perpetrators and improve our own data security. And finally, why we think national data breach notification legislation is important.

Epsilon is the leading provider of permission-based email marketing services. Our clients, some of the world's largest and best-known consumer and financial services brands count on us to send their email messages to their customers, the individual consumer. And as we all know, major brands use email messages to provide consumers with timely information about new products and sales and events, among other things. Epsilon ensures that these email messages comply with applicable legal requirements, including CAN-SPAM Act.

To earn and keep our clients' trust, Epsilon became the first in the industry in 2006 to certify that its information security program complied with the standards issued by the International Association of Standardization, known as ISO. ISO, a highly regarded organization, is recognized by over 160 countries around the world, including the United States, as identifying best practices for information security management. The standards are demanding, requiring over a year to earn initial certification. We are proud that Epsilon leads the industry and that we have achieved yearly recertification, which requires proof that the company is improving its security program each year.

Notwithstanding our internal security procedures and our compliance with these rigorous data security standards, as you know, Epsilon was the victim of a criminal hacking incident at the end of March. Since our information security program was designed to identify and respond to attacks and threats, we were quickly able to detect the unauthorized download activity, which triggered Epsilon's security incident response program.

Our investigation, both internal and with an independent third party, is coordinated closely with the Secret Service and is still ongoing. But we can say that the initial investigation confirms that only email addresses and, in some cases, first and last names were affected by this attack. Again, only email addresses and, in some cases, first and last names were affected. The details of what happened after the attack are in my written statement that has been submitted for the record. We are greatly troubled that this criminal incident has called into question our commitment to data security. But I want to leave you with four main points about what happened and how Epsilon responded.

First, our internal response to the criminal attack was immediate. We isolated computers and changed employee access rights. Second, our forensics investigation began within hours. We also reached out to law enforcement just as quickly. Third, notification to our clients also occurred on the same day, and we released a public statement and posted additional public information on our Web site shortly thereafter. And finally, now and going forward, we reiterate our commitment to working with the Secret Service, apprehending the hackers, and improving our own security.

Companies like Epsilon are on the frontlines in the fight against data theft. We also believe Congress has an important role to play in protecting consumers. To that end, Epsilon fully supports legislation that would create a uniform standard for data breach notification. The current patchwork of over 45 individual State breach notification laws is confusing. A uniform national law, on the other hand, would provide predictability and equitable protection for consumers, regardless of their State of residence.

Chairman Bono Mack, Ranking Member Butterfield, and members of the subcommittee, we look forward to working with you as the legislative process moves forward. I sincerely hope that the information I am able to provide at this hearing is helpful to the subcommittee as it considers this critical issue. Thank you.

[The prepared statement of Ms. Fitzgerald follows:]

Prepared Statement of Jeanette Fitzgerald
General Counsel
Epsilon Data Management, LLC

Before the House Committee on Energy & Commerce
Subcommittee on Commerce, Manufacturing, and Trade
U.S. House of Representatives

June 2, 2011

Chairman Bono Mack, Ranking Member Butterfield, and distinguished members of the Subcommittee, my name is Jeanette Fitzgerald and I am the General Counsel for Epsilon Data Management. Thank you for inviting me to present Epsilon's testimony on data security.

Epsilon has been asked to participate in this hearing because it has been the victim of a criminal hacking incident. Since the incident occurred, Epsilon has worked closely with the Secret Service to identify the criminals who engaged in this malicious attack. Although it is ongoing, that investigation to date has confirmed that only email addresses and, in some cases, first and last names were affected by the attack. There is currently no evidence that any other data the company maintains were compromised.

We appreciate the opportunity to testify today and look forward to an ongoing dialogue on this important subject. Epsilon supports national data breach notification legislation and stands ready to serve as a resource to this Committee as you continue to consider this critical issue.

About Epsilon

Epsilon is a leading provider of permission-based e-mail marketing services, and proudly claims as clients some of the world's largest and best-known consumer and financial service brands. The company's roots lie in the direct mail marketing industry, where for over 40 years Epsilon has provided valuable services to companies seeking to market to consumers directly through means such as catalog marketing. Today, in addition to those and other related services, Epsilon also provides many well known companies and brands with a comprehensive e-mail marketing platform. Consumers choose ("opt-in") to receive email communications from Epsilon's clients. For example, consumers may choose to provide their e-mail addresses to an Epsilon client in order to receive discounts or other special offers. Epsilon provides the mechanism through which its clients can help ensure that consumer e-mail lists are maintained and messages to them are compliant with the Controlling the Assault of Non-Solicited Pornography and Marketing Act of 2003 ("CAN-SPAM"), including managing consumer opt-out requests in the event that a consumer who has opted-in decides they no longer want to receive emails from the Epsilon client. Epsilon's e-mail platform lets its clients – and Epsilon employees acting on their behalf as account managers – manage this data.

As a provider of data management services to major consumer brands and financial institutions, Epsilon is committed to responsible information governance and recognizes the importance of keeping client data secure. To enhance security across its infrastructure, Epsilon for the past several years has implemented and maintains an information security program conforming to data security standards set forth by the International Organization for Standardization ("ISO"). More specifically, Epsilon has implemented an ISO 27001[1] compliant information security management system that implements ISO 27002[2] controls. This system requires an information security program that assesses an organization's information security risks, designs and implements comprehensive safeguards to control unacceptable risks, and

---

[1] International Organization for Standardization, ISO/IEC 27001:2005, http://www.iso.org/iso/catalogue_detail?csnumber=42103.
[2] International Organization for Standardization, ISO/IEC 27002:2005, http://www.iso.org/iso/catalogue_detail?csnumber=50297.

maintains that program to ensure continued improvement and ongoing assessments. The goal of the ISO 27002 standard is to facilitate best practices for controlling the types of information security risks to which companies like Epsilon might be exposed. Combined, the ISO 27001 standard and 27002 controls provide a process for comprehensive information security that is detailed, rigorous, and adaptable to changing circumstances.[3]

Epsilon was the first in its industry to become ISO 27001 certified. Epsilon has been ISO 27001 certified since 2006, and has subsequently received yearly re-certifications. Acquiring this certification is a thorough and demanding process. The certification process, which started in 2005, took nearly a year to complete and required validation from independent third-party auditors. Epsilon has maintained its ISO 27001 certification every year since then, undergoing yearly reviews that demand continual improvements to the company's information security program. By obtaining and maintaining this certification, Epsilon has demonstrated its commitment to ensuring that its information security program provides reasonable and appropriate safeguards for client and consumer data.

Incident Chronology

Like many other organizations, Epsilon's information security program is designed to identify and respond to attacks and threats. In identifying the recent attack on Epsilon's systems, the company's security program detected unauthorized download activity and invoked Epsilon's security incident response program. This led to an immediate move to investigate and remediate the unauthorized entry and to put in place additional safeguards based on the company's findings. The following is a brief chronology of the incident.

---

[3] Ted Humphreys, *State-of-the-Art Information Security Management Systems with ISO/IEC 27001:2005*, ISO INSIDER, Jan.-Feb., 2006, *available at* http://www.iso.org/iso/info_security.pdf.

On March 30, an Epsilon employee contacted the e-mail application support team and reported unusual download activity that seemed suspicious. The Epsilon security investigation team responded immediately, beginning an internal investigation and reaching out to federal law enforcement authorities. Epsilon's internal investigation revealed that the login credentials of the employee had been compromised. As soon as Epsilon's investigators identified the compromised credentials, the security team disabled the credentials and began a forensic investigation of the relevant computer resources. Epsilon's immediate response activities included:

- Initiating additional virus scans of relevant systems.

- Revoking and re-issuing Epsilon system-user credentials for administrator-level users.

- Committing additional resources to monitoring unusual or suspicious activity.

- Beginning a forensic investigation to identify root causes.

- Notifying law enforcement including the FBI and Secret Service to seek their assistance, which resulted in the Secret Service beginning its investigation on April 1.

In addition to efforts to identify and contain the incident within the company, Epsilon also promptly began to assist its clients. These actions included:

- Contacting potentially affected clients and cooperating with them on an ongoing basis.

- Communicating with Epsilon's anti-virus support vendor to identify threat signatures and obtain additional support.

Epsilon has also worked to help address the concerns of consumers by providing public notice of the incident on the Epsilon website on April 1[4] with an additional update on April 6[5], and has set up an incident response center to answer questions from consumers and our corporate clients. Additionally, Epsilon has added information to its website to provide consumers with educational materials on guarding against phishing attacks.[6] Specifically, this information explains what phishing attacks are, how they occur, and the steps a consumer can take to avoid becoming a victim.

On April 2, Epsilon met with its outside forensic consultants to review the evidence collected to date and confirm that information was flowing appropriately to the Secret Service. Epsilon's outside forensic consultants also reviewed the company's containment measures implemented thus far and, as the investigation unfolds, will make recommendations regarding further measures.

To date, the investigation has confirmed that only e-mail addresses and, in some cases, first and last names of consumers have been affected. At this time Epsilon has no evidence that any other data the company maintains were compromised in this attack. It appears that the attacker was only able to steal data from Epsilon's e-mail services platform; other platforms, such as its hosted client databases, were not affected. Going forward, Epsilon will continue to adhere to and improve its security policies and procedures, especially in light of this criminal

---

[4] Press Release, Epsilon, Epsilon Notifies Clients of Unauthorized Entry into Email System (Apr. 1, 2011), http://www.epsilon.com/News%20&%20Events/Press_Releases_2011/Epsilon_Notifies_Clients_of_Unauthorized_Entry_into_Email_System/p1057-l3.

[5] Press Release, Epsilon, Alliance Data Provides Statement Surrounding Unauthorized Entry Incident at Epsilon Subsidiary (Apr. 6, 2011), http://www.epsilon.com/News%20&%20Events/Press_Releases_2011/Alliance_Data_Provides_Statement_Surrounding_Unauthorized_Entry_Incident_at_Epsilon_Subsidiary/p1061-l3.

[6] Epsilon, Consumer Information on Phishing, http://www.epsilon.com/Privacy%20Policy/Consumer_Information_on_Phishing/p467-l2.

attack on its e-mail services platform. Further, Epsilon has engaged third-party experts to review and recommend additional hardening processes to the company's existing controls.

Data Breach Legislation

As the company's General Counsel, it is my job to make sure that we continue to work with law enforcement to make sure that we uncover all of the facts of this attack and to continue to improve security measures at the company every day. I am committed to doing so but also believe that Congress has an important role to play in protecting end consumers.

In this regard, Epsilon appreciates the opportunity to also provide input on potential data breach legislation being considered by the Subcommittee. Epsilon fully supports national legislation that would create a uniform standard for data breach notification. The current patchwork of individual state breach notification laws only serves to create confusion among consumers and businesses, and imposes unnecessary compliance costs. A uniform national law, on the other hand, would provide predictability and equity for consumers, regardless of their state of residence, and would make it much easier and less costly for business to ensure any applicable notification requirements are met.

Conclusion

For decades, Epsilon's commitment to trust and data security has helped the company build client relationships with some of the largest consumer and financial services brands in the world. Epsilon knows its clients, in turn, work hard to protect the privacy of consumers. For these reasons, Epsilon deeply regrets that the criminal activities of others have called into question this commitment. Epsilon is determined to investigate the unauthorized intrusion into the company's e-mail services platform thoroughly and remediate promptly and appropriately. As data management services become more sophisticated, criminals likewise are enhancing their efforts to infiltrate even the most sophisticated systems. Epsilon will continue to respond to these criminal threats – by improving its own systems and working with law enforcement to try and apprehend those responsible for this intrusion. Our ultimate goal is to ensure reasonable protections for data management, our clients, and, most importantly, the end consumers.

I sincerely hope that the information I am able to provide at this hearing is helpful to the Subcommittee. Epsilon looks forward to working with the Subcommittee to help it understand the data security challenges that companies are continually facing, and to provide input on effective data security legislation that is in the best interests of both consumers and businesses.

Thank you.

Mrs. BONO MACK. Thank you, Ms. Fitzgerald. And Mr. Schaaff, you are recognized for 5 minutes.

STATEMENT OF TIM SCHAAFF

Mr. SCHAAFF. Thank you. Chairman Bono Mack, Ranking Member Butterfield, and other distinguished members of the subcommittee, thank you for providing Sony with this opportunity to testify on cyber crime and data security.

My name is Tim Schaaff and I am president of Sony Network Entertainment International, a subsidiary of Sony Corporation based in California, where we employ approximately 700 people in five offices around the State. I am chiefly responsible for the business and technical aspects of Sony's PlayStation Network and Curiosity, an online service that allows consumers to access movies, television shows, music and video games. Sony Network Entertainment, Sony Online Entertainment—another subsidiary of Sony's—and millions of our customers were recently the victims of an increasingly common digital age crime—a cyber attack. Indeed, we have been reminded in recent days of the fact that no one is immune from the threat of cyber attack. Businesses, government entities, public institutions, and individuals can all become victims.

The attack on us, we believe, is unprecedented in its size and scope. Initially anonymous, the underground group associated with last year's WikiLeaks-related cyber attacks openly called for and carried out massive denial-of-service attacks against numerous Sony internet sites in retaliation for Sony bringing action in Federal Court to protect its intellectual property. During or shortly after those attacks, one or more highly skilled hackers infiltrated the servers of the PlayStation Network and Sony Online Entertainment.

Sony Network Entertainment and Sony Online Entertainment have always made a concerted and substantial effort to maintain and improve their data security systems. We hired a well respected and experienced cyber security firm to enhance our defenses against the denial-of-service attacks threatened by anonymous, but unfortunately, no entity can foresee every potential cyber security threat.

We have detailed for the subcommittee in our written testimony the timeline from when we first discovered the breach. But to briefly summarize, the first indication of a breach occurred on Tuesday, April 19 of this year. On Wednesday, April 20, we mobilized an investigation and immediately shut down all of the PlayStation Network services in order to prevent additional unauthorized activity. After two highly respected technical forensic firms were retained to assist in a time-consuming and complicated investigation, on Friday, April 22, we notified PlayStation Network customers via post on the PlayStation blog that an intrusion had occurred. After a third forensic firm was retained, on Monday, April 25, we were able to confirm the scope of the personal data that we believed had been accessed. And although there was no evidence credit card information had been accessed, we could not rule out the possibility.

Therefore, the very next day, Tuesday, April 26, we issued a public notice that we believed the personal information of our customers had been taken. And that while there was no evidence that credit card data was taken, since we could not rule out the possibility, we had to acknowledge that it was possible. We also posted this on our blog and began to email each of our accountholders directly. We did not merely make statements on our blog.

On Sunday, May 1, Sony Online Entertainment, a multi-player online videogame network, also discovered that data may have been taken. On Monday, May 2, just one day later, Sony Online Entertainment shut down this service and notified customers directly that their personal information may have also been compromised. Throughout this time, we felt a keen sense of responsibility to our customers. We shut down the networks to protect against further unauthorized activity. We notified our customers promptly when we had specific, accurate, and useful information. We thanked our customers for their patience and loyalty and addressed their concerns arising from this breach with identify theft protection programs for the U.S. and other customers around the world where available, as well as a welcome-back package of extended and free subscriptions, games, and other services. And we worked to restore our networks to stronger security to protect our customer's interests.

Let me address the specific issues you are considering today: notification of consumers when data breaches occur. Laws and common sense provide for companies to investigate breaches, gather the facts, and then report data losses publicly. If you reverse that order issuing vague or speculative statements before you have specific and reliable information, you either send false alarms or so many alarms that these warnings may be ignored. We therefore support federal data breach legislation and look forward to working with the subcommittee on the particulars of the bill.

One final point—as frustrating as the loss of networks for playing games was for our customers, the consequences of cyber attacks against financial or defense institutions can be devastating for our economy and security. Consider the fact that defense contractor Lockheed Martin and the Oakridge National Laboratory, which helps the Department of Energy secure the Nation's electric grid, were also cyber attacked within the past 2 months.

By working together to enact meaningful cyber security legislation, we can limit the threat posed to us all. We look forward to this initiative to make sure that consumers are empowered with the information and tools they need to protect themselves from cyber criminals. Thank you very much.

[The prepared statement of Mr. Schaaff follows:]

Opening Statement of

Tim Schaaff

President of Sony Network Entertainment International

Before the Subcommittee on Commerce, Manufacturing and Trade

of the U.S. House of Representatives Committee on Energy and Commerce

Washington, DC

June 2, 2011

Chairman Bono Mack, Ranking Member Butterfield, and other distinguished members of the Subcommittee, thank you for providing Sony with this opportunity to testify on cyber crime and data security.

My name is Tim Schaaff, and I am President of Sony Network Entertainment International, a subsidiary of Sony Corporation based in California, where we employ approximately 700 people in five offices around the state.

I am chiefly responsible for the business and technical aspects of Sony's PlayStation Network and Qriocity, online services that allow consumers to access movies, television shows, music and video games.

Sony Network Entertainment, Sony Online Entertainment and millions of our customers were recently the victims of an increasingly common digital-age crime: a cyber attack.

Indeed, we have been reminded in recent days of the fact that no one is immune from the threat of cyber attack; businesses, government entities, public institutions and individuals can all become victims.

We applaud the Subcommittee and your colleagues in Congress for your work on cyber security, and we look forward to working with you to make the Internet a safer place for everyone to learn, enjoy entertainment and engage in commerce.

The attack on us was, we believe, unprecedented in its size and scope. Initially, Anonymous, the underground group associated with last year's WikiLeaks-related cyber attacks, openly called for and carried out massive "denial-of-service" attacks against numerous Sony Internet sites in retaliation for Sony bringing an action in federal court to protect its intellectual property. During or shortly after those attacks, one or more highly skilled hackers infiltrated the servers of the PlayStation Network and Sony Online Entertainment.

Sony Network Entertainment and Sony Online Entertainment have always made concerted and substantial efforts to maintain and improve their data security systems. We hired a well-respected and experienced cyber-security firm to enhance our defenses against the denial-of-service attacks threatened by Anonymous. But unfortunately no entity – be it a mom-and-pop business, a multinational corporation, or the federal government – can foresee every potential cyber-security threat.

On Tuesday, April 19, 2011, our network team discovered unplanned and unusual activity taking place on four of the many servers that comprise the PlayStation Network. The network team took those four servers off line and an internal assessment began.

On Wednesday, April 20th, we mobilized a larger internal team to assist in the investigation. And on that date, the team discovered the first credible indications that an intruder had been attempting to access customer data in the PlayStation Network system. We immediately shut down all of the PlayStation Network services in order to prevent additional unauthorized activity.

That same afternoon, we retained a security firm to "mirror" the servers to enable a forensic analysis. The scope and complexity of the investigation grew substantially as additional evidence about the attack developed.

On Thursday, April 21st, a second recognized firm was retained to assist in the investigation.

On Friday, April 22nd, we notified PlayStation Network customers via a post on the PlayStation Blog that an intrusion had occurred. That blog, by the way, has been rated one of the top-twenty most influential on the Internet, right behind the White House's blog. It has a highly visible and deeply engaging relationship with our customers and is one of the best, fastest and most direct means of communicating with them.

By the evening of Saturday, April 23rd, we were able to confirm that intruders had used very sophisticated and aggressive techniques to obtain unauthorized access to the servers and hide their presence from the system administrators.

On Sunday, April 24th, yet another forensic team with highly specialized skills was retained to help determine the scope of the intrusion.

By Monday, April 25th, we were able to confirm the scope of the personal data that we believed had been accessed. Although there was no evidence credit card information was accessed, we could not rule out the possibility.

The very next day - Tuesday, April 26th - we issued a public notice that we believed the personal information of our customers had been taken and that, while there was no evidence that credit card data was taken, we could not rule out the possibility. We also posted this on our blog and began to email each of our account-holders directly.

On Sunday, May 1st, Sony Online Entertainment, a multiplayer, online video game network, discovered that data may have been taken. On Monday, May 2nd, Sony Online

Entertainment shut down this service and notified customers that their personal information may have been compromised.

Throughout this time, we felt a keen sense of responsibility to our customers:

- We shut down the networks to protect against further unauthorized activity.

- We notified our customers promptly when we had specific, accurate and useful information.

- We thanked our customers for their patience and loyalty and addressed their concerns arising from this breach with identity theft protection programs for US and other customers (where available) and a "Welcome Back" package of extended and free subscriptions, games and other services.

- And we worked to restore our networks with stronger security to protect our customers' interests.

Let me address the specific issue you are considering today – notification of consumers when data breaches occur. Laws – and common sense – provide for companies to investigate breaches, gather the facts, and then report data losses publicly. If you reverse that order – issuing vague or speculative statements before you have specific and reliable information – you either confuse and panic people, without giving them useful facts, or you bombard them with so many announcements that they become background noise.

As recently noted by Director of National Intelligence James Clapper, "...almost two-thirds of US firms report that they have been the victim of cyber security incidents or information breaches." So we must strike the right balance between giving people the information they need, when they need it, without sounding false alarms or so many alarms that these warnings are ignored.

We support federal data breach legislation that would: (1) provide consumers the assurance that if and when their personal data is compromised, they will receive timely, meaningful and accurate notice of this fact; (2) ensure that consumers receive helpful information on what measures they can take to mitigate any potential harm; and (3) provide uniformity so consumers are treated equally no matter what state they live in and businesses no longer have to navigate varying and sometimes seemingly conflicting state laws in this field.

One final point: as frustrating as the loss of networks for playing games was for our customers, the consequences of cyber attacks against financial or defense institutions can be devastating for our economy and security. Consider the fact that defense contractor Lockheed Martin and the Oak Ridge National Laboratory, which helps the Department of Energy secure the nation's electric grid, were cyber attacked within the past two months.

By working together to enact meaningful cyber-security legislation, we can limit the threat posed to us all. We look forward to this initiative to ensure that consumers are empowered with the information and tools they need to protect themselves from cyber criminals.

As the Subcommittee is aware, we have submitted letters responding to a variety of questions posed by the Subcommittee regarding the details of the cyber attack we experienced, and I ask that those letters be submitted as part of the record of this hearing.

Thank you.

SONY

COMPUTER
ENTERTAINMENT®

Sony Computer Entertainment America
919 East Hillsdale Blvd.
Foster City, California 94404-2175
650 655 8000
650 655 8001 Fax

May 3, 2011

The Honorable Mary Bono Mack
Chairman
Subcommittee on Commerce, Manufacturing, and Trade
United States Congress
2125 Rayburn House Office Building
Washington, D.C. 20515

The Honorable G. K. Butterfield
Ranking Member
Subcommittee on Commerce, Manufacturing, and Trade
United States Congress
2125 Rayburn House Office Building
Washington, D.C. 20515

Dear Chairman Bono Mack and Ranking Member Butterfield:

Thank you for giving me this opportunity to respond to questions from the House Energy and Commerce Committee, Subcommittee on Commerce, Manufacturing and Trade.

Sony now faces a large-scale cyber-attack involving the theft of personal information. This cyber-attack came shortly after Sony Computer Entertainment America was the subject of denial of service attacks launched against several Sony companies and threats made against both Sony and its executives in retaliation for enforcing intellectual property rights in U.S. Federal Court. We are currently dealing with all aspects of this cyber-attack and have our personnel deployed and working around the clock to get the systems back up and to make sure all our customers are informed of the data breach and our responses to it. We expect to restore most services to our customers shortly. We have received so far no confirmed reports of illegal usage of the stolen information.

In dealing with this cyber-attack, the company has operated on the basis of several key principles:

1.   Act with care and caution. This is why Sony Network Entertainment America Inc. ("Sony Network Entertainment America"), which operates the PlayStation Network and Qriocity services (collectively, "PlayStation Network"), has taken the almost unprecedented step of shutting down the affected systems as soon as threats were detected and is keeping them down, even at substantial cost to the company, until all changes to strengthen security are completed. We have tried to err on the side of safety and security in making these decisions and judgments.

2.   Provide relevant information to the public when it has been verified. Sony Network Entertainment America immediately hired a highly regarded information technology security firm and supplemented that firm with additional expertise and resources over several days. Sony Network Entertainment America then released information to its consumers when we and those experts believed that information was sufficiently confirmed. The truth is that retracing the steps of experienced cyber-

attackers is a highly complex process that takes time to carry out effectively. At the same time that the experienced attackers were carrying out their attack, they also attempted to destroy the evidence that would reveal their steps.

3. <u>Take responsibility for our obligations to our customers</u>. We have apologized for the inconvenience caused by the illegal intrusion into our systems and offered a free month of service in addition to the number of days the systems are down as part of a "Welcome Back" program for our customers. We are also offering our customers in the U.S. complimentary identity theft protection services.

4. <u>Work with law enforcement authorities to assist in the apprehension of those responsible and cooperate with all authorities on meeting our regulatory requirements</u>. One of our first calls was to the FBI, and this is an active, on-going investigation.

I am of course aware of the criticism Sony has received for the time taken to disclose information to our customers. I hope you can appreciate the extraordinary nature of the events the company was facing - brought on by a criminal hacker whose activity was neither immediately nor easily ascertainable. I believe that after you review all the facts you will agree that the company has been acting in good faith to release reliable information in accordance with its legal and ethical responsibilities to its valued customers.

We have been investigating this intrusion around the clock since we discovered it, and that investigation continues today. Just this past Sunday, May 1st, we learned that a likely theft from another Sony company's online service had previously gone undetected, even after highly trained technical teams had examined the network infrastructure that had been attacked around the same time as the PlayStation Network. What is becoming more and more evident is that Sony has been the victim of a very carefully planned, very professional, highly sophisticated criminal cyber attack designed to steal personal and credit card information for illegal purposes. Sunday's discovery that data had been stolen from Sony Online Entertainment only highlights this point.

When Sony Online Entertainment discovered this past Sunday afternoon that data from its servers had been stolen, it also discovered that the intruders had planted a file on one of those servers named "Anonymous" with the words "We are Legion." Just weeks before, several Sony companies had been the target of a large-scale, coordinated denial of service attack by the group called Anonymous. The attacks were coordinated against Sony as a protest against Sony for exercising its rights in a civil action in the United States District Court in San Francisco against a hacker.

While protecting individuals' personal data is the highest priority, ensuring that the Internet can be made secure for commerce is also essential. Worldwide, countries and businesses will have to come together to ensure the safety of commerce over the Internet and also find ways to combat cybercrime and cyber terrorism.

Almost two weeks ago, one or more cyber criminals gained access to PlayStation Network servers at or around the same time that these servers were experiencing denial of service attacks. The Sony Network Entertainment America team did not immediately detect the criminal intrusion for several possible reasons. First, detection was difficult because of the sheer sophistication of the intrusion. Second, detection was difficult because the criminal hackers exploited a system software vulnerability. Finally, our security teams were working very hard to defend against denial of service attacks, and that may have made it more difficult to detect this intrusion quickly – all perhaps by design.

Whether those who participated in the denial of services attacks were conspirators or whether they were simply duped into providing cover for a very clever thief, we may never know. In any case, those who participated in the denial of service attacks should understand that - whether they knew it or not - they were aiding in a well planned, well executed, large-scale theft that left not only Sony a victim, but also Sony's many customers around the world.

Making the Internet safe for entertainment, commerce and education is a paramount government interest. The criminal cyber-attacks on Sony have been and will continue to be perpetrated on other companies as well. If not addressed, these types of attacks could become commonplace. Creating more stringent guidelines for maintaining and policing storage of personal information may be necessary in our current climate, but, make no mistake, without addressing the need for strong criminal laws and sanctions and, most importantly, enforcement of these laws, there will not be any meaningful security on the Internet.

Sony is grateful for the assistance it has received from law enforcement and appreciates this opportunity to raise these issues with this Committee as it considers how to build an environment where social networks and commerce on the Internet can develop uninhibited by security risks.

Turning to Sony's responses to the Committee's questions:

1. When did you become aware of the illegal and unauthorized intrusion?

On April 19, 2011 at 4:15 p.m. PDT, members of the Sony Network Entertainment America network team detected unauthorized activity in the network system, specifically, that certain systems were re-booting when they were not scheduled to do so. The network service team immediately began to evaluate this activity by reviewing running logs and analyzing information in order to determine if there was a problem with the system.

On April 20, 2011, in the early afternoon, the Sony Network Entertainment America team discovered evidence that indicated an unauthorized intrusion had occurred and that data of some kind had been transferred off the PlayStation Network servers without authorization. At the time, the network service team was unable to determine what type of data had been transferred, and they therefore shut the PlayStation Network system down.

2. How did you become aware of the breach?

Sony Network Entertainment America became aware of the PlayStation Network intrusion as described above. The Sony Network Entertainment America team became aware of a transfer of data out of the system also as described above. Sony Network Entertainment America then began the exhaustive and highly sophisticated process of identifying the means of access and the nature and scope of the theft. That investigation is on-going to this day.

3. When did you notify the appropriate authorities of the breach?

On April 22, 2011, Sony Computer Entertainment America's general counsel provided the FBI with information about the intrusion. (Sony Computer Entertainment America oversees the PlayStation brand in North America and has been involved with the PlayStation Network's operation since its inception). The forensic experts that Sony Network Entertainment America had retained had not determined the scope or effect of the intrusion at the time the FBI was contacted. A meeting was set up to provide details to law enforcement for Wednesday April 27, 2011.

Following an extensive investigation by a team of external forensic computer experts with the assistance of the internal network service team, Sony Network Entertainment America and Sony Computer Entertainment America coordinated to provide public notice of the intrusion on April 26, 2011. On the same day, Sony Network Entertainment America notified the applicable regulatory authorities in the states of New Jersey, Maryland, and New Hampshire. On April 27, 2011, Sony Network Entertainment America also notified regulatory authorities in the states of Hawaii, Louisiana, Maine, Massachusetts, Missouri, New York, North Carolina, South Carolina, Virginia and Puerto Rico of the criminal intrusion described above.

4. Why did you wait to notify your customers of the breach?

The PlayStation Network is a complex network, consisting of approximately 130 servers, 50 software programs and 77 million registered accounts. The basic facts of what occurred after the intrusion bear this out.

On April 19, 2011, the Sony Network Entertainment America network team discovered that several PlayStation Network servers unexpectedly rebooted themselves and that unplanned and unusual activity was taking place on the network. This activity triggered an investigation. The network team took four servers off line and an internal assessment began. The internal assessment of these four servers continued through the end of the business day and into the evening. The next day, April 20th, Sony Network Entertainment America mobilized a larger internal team to assist the investigation of the four suspect servers. This internal team discovered the first credible indications that an intruder had been in the PlayStation Network systems, and six more servers were identified as possibly being compromised. Sony Network Entertainment America immediately decided to shut down all of the PlayStation Network services.

In the afternoon of April 20th, Sony Network Entertainment America retained a recognized security and forensic consulting firm to mirror the servers to enable forensic analysis to begin. The type of mirroring required to provide meaningful information in this type of situation had to be meticulous. Many hours were needed simply to mirror servers before analysis could begin. Sony Network Entertainment America and its outside forensics team began to work on mirroring the servers.

The scope and complexity of the investigation grew substantially as additional evidence about the attack developed. On April 21, 2011, Sony retained a second recognized computer security and forensic consulting firm to assist in the investigation, to provide more manpower to image the servers and to conduct a forensic analysis of all aspects of the suspected security breach.

The team took until the afternoon of April 22, 2011 to complete the mirroring of nine of the 10 servers that were suspected of being compromised. By the evening of April 23, 2011, the forensic teams were able to confirm that intruders had used very sophisticated and aggressive techniques to obtain unauthorized access, hide their presence from system administrators, and escalate privileges inside the servers. Among other things, the intruders deleted log files in order to hide the extent of their work and activity within the network. Now Sony Network Entertainment America knew it was dealing with a sophisticated hacker and (on Easter Sunday) decided that it needed to retain yet another forensic team with highly specialized skills to assist with the investigation. Specifically, this firm was retained to provide even more manpower for forensic analysis in all aspects of the suspected security breach, and, in particular, to use their special skills to determine the scope of the data theft. By April 25, 2011, the forensic teams were able to confirm the scope of the personal data that they believed had been taken but could not rule out whether credit card information had been accessed.

Sony Network Entertainment America was of course aware of its affirmative obligations under various state statutes to conduct a reasonable and prompt investigation to determine the scope of breach and depth of the breach and to restore the integrity of our network system. Sony Network Entertainment America further understood its obligation to report its finding to consumers if certain, specific kinds of personal information could have been compromised. As this Committee knows, there are a variety of state statutes that apply and several that have conflicting or inconsistent requirements, but given the global nature of the network, Sony Network Entertainment America needed to be mindful of them all. Throughout the process, Sony Network Entertainment America was very concerned that announcing partial or tentative information to consumers could cause confusion and lead them to take unnecessary actions if the information was not fully corroborated by forensic evidence. For example, as of April 25, 2011, Sony had not and could not determine if credit card information had been accessed and, while no evidence existed at the time that this type of information had been taken, we ultimately could not rule out that possibility entirely based on the reports of the forensics teams. Given that situation, on April 26, 2011, Sony Network Entertainment America and Sony Computer Entertainment America notified consumers that their personal information had been taken and that the companies could not rule out the possibility that credit card data had been stolen as well.

5. Was the information obtained applicable to all accounts or a portion of the accounts? How many consumers or accounts were impacted by this breach, and how did you ascertain the number?

Information appears to have been stolen from all PlayStation Network user accounts, although not every piece of information in those accounts appears to have been stolen. The criminal intruders stole personal information from all of the approximately 77 million PlayStation Network and Qriocity service accounts.

6. Have you identified how the breach occurred?

Yes, we believe so. Sony Network Entertainment America is continuing its investigation into this criminal intrusion, and more detailed information could be discovered during this process. We are reluctant to make full details publicly available because the information is the subject of an on-going criminal investigation and also the information could be used to exploit vulnerabilities in systems other than Sony's that have similar architecture to the PlayStation Network.

7. Have you identified the individual(s) responsible for the breach?

No.

8. What information was obtained by the unauthorized individual(s) as a result of this breach, and how did you ascertain this information?

Based on the activity of the intruder, we know that queries were made in the PlayStation Network system database for user account information related to name, address (city, state, zip), country, email address, birthdate, PlayStation Network/Qriocity password and login, and handle/PlayStation Network online ID.

As of today, the major credit card companies have not reported that they have seen any increase in the number of fraudulent credit card transactions as a result of the attack, and they have not reported to us any fraudulent transactions that they believe are a direct result of the intrusions described above.

9. How many PlayStation Network account holders provided credit card information to Sony Computer Entertainment?

Globally, approximately 12.3 million account holders had credit card information on file on the PlayStation Network system. In the United States, approximately 5.6 million account holders had credit card information on file on the system. These numbers include active and expired credit cards.

10. Your statement indicated you have no evidence at this time that credit card information was obtained, yet you cannot rule out this possibility. Please explain why you do not believe credit card information was obtained and why you cannot determine if the data was in fact taken.

As stated above, Sony Network Entertainment America has not been able to conclude with certainty through the forensic analysis done to date that credit card information was not transferred from the PlayStation Network system. We know that for other personal information contained in the account database, the hacker made queries to the database, and the external forensics teams have seen large amounts of data transferred in response to those queries. Our forensics teams have not seen queries and corresponding data transfers of the credit card information.

11. What steps have you taken or do you plan to take to prevent future such breaches.

The new security measures being implemented include the following:

- Added automated software monitoring and configuration management to help defend against new attacks;

- Enhanced levels of data protection and encryption;

- Enhanced ability to detect software intrusions within the network, unauthorized access and unusual activity patterns;

- Implementation of additional firewalls; and

- The company also expedited a planned move of the system to a new data center in a different location with enhanced security.

- The naming of new Chief Information Security Officer (CISO) directly reporting to the Chief Information Officer, Sony Corporation.

-

12. Do you currently have a policy that addresses data security and retention practices? If not, why not? If so, what are those practices and do you plan any changes in your policies as a result of this breach?

Yes, we do have policies that address data security and retention practices.

Sony utilizes a global framework for providing policies to its group companies based on the international information security standard called "ISO/IEC 27001" to ensure consistent standard information security practices for each operating company. The Global Information Security Policy ("GISP") sets forth the company's information security management structure and administrative, technical and physical safeguards to protect the confidentiality, integrity, and availability of non-public information. The GISP also defines the overall direction and policy of Sony Group's information security program and the authorities and responsibilities for information security management. Additionally, Sony provides a set of 14 standards, Global Information Security Standards ("GISS"), that specify the types of controls needed for the different categories of information security management (e.g., information classification, access controls and HR security).

Continued application of these policies and practices, in addition to, an expedited move to our new enhanced security data facility, are the changes being made as a result of this breach.

13.   What steps have you taken or do you plan to take to mitigate the effects of this breach? Do you plan to offer any credit monitoring or other services to consumers who suffer actual harm as a result of this breach?

Sony Network Entertainment America is committed to helping its customers protect their personal data and will offer its U.S. account holders complimentary identity theft protection services. Because the breach affects customers worldwide, different programs may be offered in other territories.

Sony Network Entertainment America is also creating a "Welcome Back" program to be offered worldwide, which will be tailored to specific markets to provide our consumers with a selection of service options and premium content as an expression of the company's appreciation for their patience and support.

Central components of the "Welcome Back" program will include:

- Each territory will be offering selected PlayStation entertainment content for free download. Specific details of this content will be announced in each region soon.

- All consumers coming back to the PlayStation Network will be provided with 30 days of free membership in the PlayStation Plus premium subscription service. Current PlayStation Plus subscribers will have their subscriptions extended for the number of days PlayStation Network and Qriocity services were unavailable and, in addition, will receive 30 days of free service.

- Music Unlimited subscribers (in countries where the service is available) will have their subscriptions extended for the number of days PlayStation Network and Qriocity services were unavailable and, in addition, receive 30 days of free service.

* * * *

I want to thank this Committee for giving me this opportunity to respond to its questions. I hope I have been able to convey the extraordinary circumstances and challenges that have confronted the employees of Sony Network Entertainment America and Sony Computer Entertainment America over the past few days and weeks. My employees were facing and have endured an unprecedented large-scale criminal cyber-attack. They were faced with very difficult decisions and often-times conflicting concerns and objectives. Throughout this challenging period, they acted carefully and cautiously and strove to provide correct and accurate information while balancing concerns for our consumers' privacy and need for information.

This Committee is rightfully concerned to protect the information and privacy of individuals on the Internet and to ensure that companies have robust security and protection practices. We ask the Committee to consider as well the connection between data security and the cybercrimes and cyber terrorism that threaten to make the Internet unsafe for consumers and commerce. We very much appreciate the Committee's efforts to put in place laws to protect us from these very real threats.

Respectfully submitted,

RRR for Kazuo Hirai

Kazuo Hirai
Chairman of the Board of Directors
Sony Computer Entertainment America LLC

cc: The Honorable Fred Upton
         Chairman
         U.S. House of Representatives
         Committee on Energy and Commerce

         The Honorable Henry A. Waxman
         Ranking Member
         U.S. House of Representatives
         Committee on Energy and Commerce

SONY

Sony Computer Entertainment America
919 East Hillsdale Blvd.
Foster City, California 94404-2175
650 655 8000
650 655 8001 Fax

COMPUTER
ENTERTAINMENT®

May 27, 2011

The Honorable Mary Bono Mack
Chairman
Subcommittee on Commerce, Manufacturing, and Trade
United States Congress
2125 Rayburn House Office Building
Washington, D.C. 20515

The Honorable G. K. Butterfield
Ranking Member
Subcommittee on Commerce, Manufacturing, and Trade
United States Congress
2125 Rayburn House Office Building
Washington, D.C. 20515

Dear Chairman Bono Mack and Ranking Member Butterfield:

Please find a revised copy of Kazuo Hirai's letter of May 26, 2011. The only revision was to correct the number 26.4 million in response to question 2 on page 3. The number is incorrect. The correct number of Sony Online Entertainment user accounts is approximately 24.6 million. We apologize for this typographical error and would request that this corrected version of our letter be exchanged with the original letter that is posted on the Committee's website.

Respectfully submitted,

Riley R. Russell
General Counsel
Sony Computer Entertainment America

cc: The Honorable Fred Upton
        Chairman
        U.S. House of Representatives
        Committee on Energy and Commerce

        The Honorable Henry A. Waxman
        Ranking Member
        U.S. House of Representatives
        Committee on Energy and Commerce

SONY

Sony Computer Entertainment America
919 East Hillsdale Blvd.
Foster City, California 94404-2175
650 655 8000
650 655 8001 Fax

COMPUTER
ENTERTAINMENT®

May 26, 2011

The Honorable Mary Bono Mack
Chairman
Subcommittee on Commerce, Manufacturing, and Trade
United States Congress
2125 Rayburn House Office Building
Washington, D.C. 20515

The Honorable G. K. Butterfield
Ranking Member
Subcommittee on Commerce, Manufacturing, and Trade
United States Congress
2125 Rayburn House Office Building
Washington, D.C. 20515

Dear Chairman Bono Mack and Ranking Member Butterfield:

Thank you for your letter of May 17, 2011, providing Sony with an opportunity to update our previous responses and to answer the Committee's follow-up questions. I would also like to take this opportunity to express my sincere gratitude to the committee for its appreciation of the gravity of the situation that Sony faced and, accordingly, allowing Sony to defer an appearance before the Committee. Sony was unable to appear before the Committee due to exigent circumstances. Sony was under attack, and it was critically important that our key personnel remain available and ready to address critical issues as our network and game service operations were preparing to come back on line.

To answer the Committee's questions I believe that it would be helpful to provide additional background information so that the Committee can better understand the nature and complexity of these events. Sony was the victim of multiple cyber attacks that occurred over a period of several weeks. Initially, Anonymous openly called for and carried out massive "denial of service" attacks against numerous Sony internet sites in retaliation for Sony Computer Entertainment America bringing an action in Federal Court to protect its intellectual property. The bulk of those attacks were targeted at services offered by Sony Network Entertainment America (SNEA) and Sony Online Entertainment (SOE). Many of the attacks lasted for several days. We now know that at some time during or shortly after those attacks, one or more highly skilled hackers infiltrated the servers of SNEA and SOE. The first indication that there was a problem was when several of SNEA's servers began to act in an unexpected manner. Four servers were initially isolated as suspect. As similar abnormalities were discovered in other servers within the network system, the decision to shut down the entire system was made. This was done in an attempt to protect our customers' data. At the time we did not know the cause of the abnormalities or the extent of the intrusion. Until we had more information about what had occurred, it would have been imprudent to publicly speculate about the details of the attack.

Immediately after the network was shut down, forensic experts were called in to preserve evidence so that Sony could determine what had occurred. Unfortunately the need to capture and protect evidence through the "mirroring" process often conflicts with the equally important need to understand what occurred and the scope of a breach. Information security experts could not begin to understand what had happened, or the scope of the breach, until they had captured all the data on the affected servers. This takes time. More problematic, evidence shows that the hacker(s) took measures to cover their tracks in and out of the servers and to conceal what information they stole. Our forensic investigation is still ongoing and definitive answers remain elusive. As yet, we do not know who was responsible for the intrusion; nor do we know precisely the amount of information that was taken; nor do we know with certainty the number of users whose data was actually affected. These gaps in what we know are not for lack of trying by experts, but rather an unfortunate testament to the skill of those who perpetrated the attacks. Some aspects of the intrusion may never be known. To date, however, there is no evidence that credit card information was taken.

One final point before turning to your questions: we are very reluctant to release certain investigative information publicly because it is the subject of an ongoing criminal investigation, and because its disclosure could jeopardize the security of other network systems, not just our own. If the Committee wishes technical specifics, we would be happy to explore ways in which we could share this information with you – either under seal or in camera – if such means are available. In answering the Committee's questions, where appropriate I have noted these concerns. Turning to your questions:

1) **Has your investigation revealed any additional information on what customer information was specifically obtained, and whether the information was obtained from all accounts or a portion of the accounts?**

   We have information that suggests what the hacker was accessing and what the hacker may have downloaded, but we are unable to determine conclusively whether information was actually taken from all or just a portion of the user accounts. Accordingly, we believe it is appropriate for notification purposes to assume information could have been taken from any of the 77 million accounts, and we have notified each of our account holders using e-mail and/or public notices.

Letter to Honorable Mary Bono Mack &
Honorable G. K. Butterfield
May 26, 2011
Page 3 of 6

2) **When Sony representatives briefed our staff on May 3, 2011, they indicated that personal information from all 77 million accounts had been breached in some form. In your May 3, 2011 response to our letter you indicated not every piece of information in each account had been stolen, but that some personal information on all 77 million had been stolen. Has your investigation revealed what information was taken from each individual account? Do you have any additional information that would call for revising the number of affected accounts?**

To answer this question accurately it is necessary to distinguish between SNEA and SOE.

The 77 million user accounts referenced by our representatives referred to all of the SNEA customer accounts. Available evidence suggests that a database containing personal information for every account was accessed and that an attempt was made to take information from certain data fields in that database. We advised all of our customers in e-mails and on our website that we believed: *"an unauthorized person has obtained the following information that you provided: name, address (city, state, zip), country, email address, birthdate, PlayStation Network/Qriocity password and login, and handle/PSN online ID."* This list reflected the information we know the hacker accessed and was the data the hacker attempted to take off the servers. Unfortunately we cannot confirm whether the hacker was completely successful in taking all of that information off the servers, or just a subset of it; in an abundance of caution, Sony advised all of its customers that it believed that the data had been obtained.

On May 1, 2011, SOE discovered that customer data on its servers had also been accessed in a manner very similar to the SNEA intrusion. SOE gave notice of the breach to all of its customers. SOE had approximately 24.6 million user accounts containing user information.

3) **Has your investigation revealed how the breach occurred?**

We believe we know how the hacker gained access to each of the two networks, but the investigation is ongoing regarding other aspects of the criminal attack. As stated above, we believe that publically releasing these facts could jeopardize the ongoing investigation and potentially put other network systems at risk. We would be happy to explore a confidential and secure manner in which to outline this information to the Committee.

4) **Your initial reply to us on May 3 indicated the attack may have been coordinated and directed by the group of cyber criminals named 'Anonymous'. Have you identified those who are responsible for the breach, including any individual (s)?**

Letter to Honorable Mary Bono Mack &
Honorable G. K. Butterfield
May 26, 2011
Page 4 of 6

We have not yet identified the individual or individuals responsible for the actual intrusion and breach into our systems. We are continuing to work with the FBI to apprehend those responsible.

5) **When our staffs met on May 3, 2011, your representatives indicated Sony could not confirm whether credit card information had been breached but, at the time, there was no evidence to indicate that such information had been breached. Has your investigation revealed any additional information regarding whether credit card information was indeed taken.**

Based on the evidence available on May 3, 2011, Sony believed that no credit card data had been taken from PSN/Qriocity but could not rule it out. Since that time, no further forensic or circumstantial evidence has been discovered to suggest that any credit card data was taken. In addition, to date there have been no confirmed reports of credit card misuse or reports of an increase in fraudulent transactions resulting from this incident. Even so, our investigation is continuing.

6) **Sony discovered on May 1 that an additional breach of its network occurred. This breach reportedly involved approximately 25 million user accounts at Sony Online Entertainment**

a. **Was this breach the same as, related to, or unrelated to the Sony PlayStation Network breach? Have you identified the responsible party?**

The timing, techniques, and methods used by the hacker suggest that the SOE breach was perpetrated by the same person or persons as the PlayStation Network breach. We have not yet identified the responsible party.

b. **When did the breach occur? If there was a delay in the discovery of the Sony Online Entertainment breach, what was the reason for the delay?**

Until May 1, 2011, SOE did not believe that any data had been taken from its databases, but access to the database appears to have occurred on April 16th and 17th, 2011. Upon learning that its databases had been breached, SOE made an announcement to its customers the following day. The investigation is continuing.

7) **What steps has Sony taken or does Sony plan to take to mitigate the effects of these breaches on its customers?**

Sony is making identity theft insurance available to customers in the United States. These customers are being offered a one year, $1 million identity theft insurance policy. Similar

programs will be offered in Canada and in the Latin American countries where such programs
are available. In countries where insurance is not available, Sony is seeking to identify
comparable programs to offer to its customers. In addition, while much of the PlayStation
network is a free service, services on the PlayStation Network or Qriocity service that are fee
based will be extended for the period of time that the service was down. For all of Sony's
network customers, Sony is offering a "Welcome Back" package that provides several free
offers including our Music Unlimited and PlayStation Plus services (for PlayStation owners) for a
period of 30 days, along with a multitude of other free offerings.

8) **Regarding both the Sony PlayStation Network and the Sony Online Entertainment servers,
you indicated in your May 3 response steps Sony is implementing to prevent future such
breaches. Do you believe these additional security measures will prevent future breaches or
illegal intrusions? Why did you not have these measures in place prior to the breach(es)?**

Sony took aggressive action to contain the intrusion and believes that its enhanced security
measures should improve the security of these networks against attempted breaches in the
future. We also recognize that no security system is absolutely foolproof, and changing
conditions in the future can make a currently secure environment less secure: security is a
never-ending battle of measures, counter-measures and counter-counter-measures against
rapidly evolving and new threats. In light of this, SNEA and SOE now have an ongoing program
of updating technology, continual testing of their security systems, review of external threats,
and cooperation with law enforcement to provide a safe environment for customers. SNEA
was in the process of putting in place several key security measures (as set out in my May 3
response) before the attacks occurred; SOE had already taken a variety of steps in a multi-
layered approach to securing its network prior to the attack. In light of the sophistication of the
attack, each company has made further refinements to its overall network security including
new intrusion detection methods, policy changes, additional firewall protection, and more in-
depth application testing prior to deployment.

9) **Did Sony have a policy in place at the time of either breach addressing data security and data
retention practices? If not, why not? If so, what are those practices and does Sony plan any
changes in its policies as a result of this breach?**

Sony has several policies addressing data security. Both companies were covered by the
company's Global Information Security Policy, Global Information Security Standards, and the
Global Basic Principles On Personal Information. Each company had its own privacy and IT
security officers. In addition, SNEA and SOE are substantially building up their network security
by increasing the number of technical measures they employ; for SNEA, the company has
moved its data center to a more secure facility and, in light of this incident, SNEA and SOE are

Letter to Honorable Mary Bono Mack &
Honorable G. K. Butterfield
May 26, 2011
Page 6 of 6

reviewing their policies for scheduled inspection and updating of their sites. Moreover, both companies are conducting reviews on numerous fronts to help assure both procedural and substantive best practices going forward.

10) **In today's Wall Street Journal, Chief Executive Howard Stringer said Sony "can't guarantee the security of its videogame network… in the bad new world of cyber crime". Please explain what he meant, as well as the potential impact on consumers.**

Mr. Stringer sought to emphasize that no individual, corporation, or government entity, standing alone, can truly guarantee security in a world of very sophisticated hackers, cyber attacks, and cyber terrorism. Sony is implementing better and more robust security measures to protect our customers. But just as individuals and businesses have come to rely on multiple law enforcement agencies for physical protection, we believe the private sector will need the assistance and support of government and law enforcement to help secure e-commerce and IT systems to stay ahead of and curtail the activity of cyber criminals and cyber terrorists.

We hope this letter assists the Committee in answering the questions that it has posed.

Respectfully submitted,

RRR for Kazuo Hirai

Kazuo Hirai
Chairman of the Board of Directors
Sony Computer Entertainment America LLC

cc: The Honorable Fred Upton
        Chairman
        U.S. House of Representatives
        Committee on Energy and Commerce

        The Honorable Henry A. Waxman
        Ranking Member
        U.S. House of Representatives
        Committee on Energy and Commerce

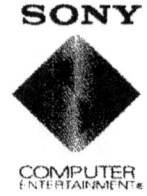

SONY

COMPUTER
ENTERTAINMENT®

Sony Computer Entertainment America
919 East Hillsdale Blvd.
Foster City, California 94404-2175
650 655 8000
650 655 8001 Fax

May 31, 2011

The Honorable Mary Bono Mack
Chairman
Subcommittee on Commerce, Manufacturing, and Trade
United States Congress
2125 Rayburn House Office Building
Washington, D.C. 20515

The Honorable G. K. Butterfield
Ranking Member
Subcommittee on Commerce, Manufacturing, and Trade
United States Congress
2125 Rayburn House Office Building
Washington, D.C. 20515

Dear Chairman Bono Mack and Ranking Member Butterfield:

In reviewing our recent letter, we realized that it did not separately restate questions 6c, 6d, or 6e. Although the answers to those questions were largely subsumed in answers to other questions, in order to avoid confusion at the hearing, we felt it would be useful to supplement our response. Our answers are as follows:

> **6) c. How many user accounts were impacted?**
>
> Approximately 24.6 million user accounts were affected.
>
> **6) d. What information was taken?**
>
> The user information that we believe was taken was: name, country code, email address, birthdate, hashed password and login name. In addition, there is evidence that the name, email address and physical address of 16 customers and that the name/address and telephone number of one customer may have also been accessed.
>
> **6) e. When did Sony notify its Sony Online Entertainment users that their accounts had been breached?**

Letter to Honorable Mary Bono Mack &
Honorable G. K. Butterfield
May 26, 2011
Page 2 of 2

Sony Online Entertainment learned that its databases had been breached on May 1, and made an announcement to its customers the following day. The investigation is continuing.

We hope that this supplemental letter avoids any confusion. Thank you.

Respectfully submitted,

Riley R. Russell
General Counsel
Sony Computer Entertainment America LLC

cc: The Honorable Fred Upton
Chairman
U.S. House of Representatives
Committee on Energy and Commerce

The Honorable Henry A. Waxman
Ranking Member
U.S. House of Representatives
Committee on Energy and Commerce

Mrs. BONO MACK. Thank you, Mr. Schaaff. And I would like to thank both of you for your opening statements, as well as for your unique insight into these disturbing data breaches. I am confident that the lessons learned with assist us in our efforts to develop new online safeguards for American consumers.

And I am going to recognize myself for the first 5 minutes of questioning.

And, Mr. Schaaff, given the extreme makeover of Sony's online security protocols, it does beg the question why weren't many of these safeguards, such as having a chief security information officer in place before the April data breaches?

Mr. SCHAAFF. We believe that the security that we had in place was very, very strong and we felt that we were in good shape. However, as the attacks indicated, the intensity and sophistication of the hack was such that even despite those best measures that we had taken, it was not sufficient. And as we recognize moving forward that the scrutiny that we are likely to be under from the hackers will continue, we have made additional commitments to enhance the security of our networks.

In addition, we had been working for some months now, more than 18 months to expand both the capacity and security of our network. We are a new business but we are a very fast-growing business.

Mrs. BONO MACK. All right. Let me jump ahead.

Mr. SCHAAFF. Sure.

Mrs. BONO MACK. You indicated with Sony in the May 3 letter that you contacted the FBI on April 22, which was 2 days after it determined the breach had in fact occurred. Why did Sony wait 2 days to notify law enforcement?

Mr. SCHAAFF. My understanding is that we notified them as soon as we had something clear that we could report that indicated some sign of external intrusion that would be unauthorized or illegal.

Mrs. BONO MACK. Your testimony indicates four servers were taken offline on April 19 before you pulled the plug on all 130 servers. Can you tell us what information was different that was stored on those initial four servers?

Mr. SCHAAFF. Well, these were part of a larger network of machines and we believed this was just the first entry point that the hacker may have used to get into the network, and upon discovering them, we immediately shut them down. But there were other servers that were also attacked by the hackers as well.

Mrs. BONO MACK. Some media reports indicate Sony's servers may not have had up-to-date patches or firewalls prior to the attack. Is that true?

Mr. SCHAAFF. That is actually patently false. The Apache servers were fully up to date, fully patched. And in fact, we had had several layers of firewalls in place, also contrary to so many of the things you may have read on the internet. As you know, the internet is not always a reliable source of factual information.

Mrs. BONO MACK. And you state that you believe the cyber attack on Sony was unprecedented in both size and scope. Can you explain why you believe it is unprecedented?

Mr. SCHAAFF. Well, we believe that the sophistication of the attack, the collection of activities that were undertaken, the period of time in which the hackers were carefully exploring the network, and then ultimately the scope of the service that was breached makes it quite a remarkable attack. And despite the deep security measures that we had taken, it was nevertheless insufficient to guard against these attacks.

Mrs. BONO MACK. Was the consumer data you held encrypted? And why or why not?

Mr. SCHAAFF. So, of course, the credit card information that was held was encrypted. Password login data was protected using cryptographic hash functions. And these practices are in line with industry practice.

Mrs. BONO MACK. Thank you. Ms. Fitzgerald, would greater security requirements have prevented your breach? And if not, what added protection are your new security measures providing?

Ms. FITZGERALD. At the time, we had very extensive security as I noted in my opening statement and the written statement I provided. We have continued through the investigation to evaluate additional things that may be done to strengthen both our networks and any of the access points. We have also decided to hire some outside experts to even evaluate the network further and see if there is anything else in different parts of our network that need to be adjusted.

Mrs. BONO MACK. Coming as a consumer who received multiple notices about your breach, there are also indications that consumers received notice of the breach from your business customers for which, in some cases, they hadn't had a purchase or customer relationship for 4 or 5 years. Do you ever purge your data and why do you hold onto information for as long as you do?

Ms. FITZGERALD. So let me step back a second to remind everyone how Epsilon plays in this. Epsilon is a service provider to the well-known names that you may have received notifications from, and they have the relationship with the consumer. What data we hold is determined by the client, and the client then tells us what to hold and what we then do with it in terms of sending out notices or any sort of marketing messages is entirely up to the client. It is not——

Mrs. BONO MACK. Do you advise them on when it might be a good time to purge data?

Ms. FITZGERALD. It depends on what they want to do with the data. And there is also opt-out data that would have been held because in order to comply with CAN–SPAM, you have to maintain records of who has opted out. So if, 2 years ago, you opted out and you haven't had any activity, that list would still be there because you have to comply with CAN–SPAM. So we have to be able to duplicate or de-duplicate and take those names out any time that we do a mailing.

Mrs. BONO MACK. OK. Thank you. My time has expired. I will recognize the ranking member, Mr. Butterfield, for his 5 minutes.

Mr. BUTTERFIELD. Thank you, Madam Chairman.

Mr. Schaaff, let me start with you and if I have any time remaining, I will go over to Ms. Fitzgerald.

Mr. Schaaff, I understand that your internal investigation has not turned up any evidence suggesting that credit card data was taken from the network, but to me, that doesn't necessarily mean that the data was not taken, just that you haven't turned up any digital fingerprints that would allow you to know with certainty that it was taken. And I think you see what I am saying there. Help me with that. How certain are you that the data was not taken in the attack?

Mr. SCHAAFF. Well, as you know, we have been engulfed in an intensive investigation over the past 6 weeks since the breach occurred, and we have looked deeply at the logs related to the databases. And in those logs we have found no clear evidence that there was any access made to the credit card information, and we found plenty of evidence that suggests that that data was not accessed. That is the basis for today's statements that we do not believe the credit card information was compromised.

Mr. BUTTERFIELD. Now, in your testimony, you mentioned that the attack took place on April 19, that the PlayStations were shut down on April 20, and that you did something on April 22. Help me with that if you could shed some light on what you did on April 22.

Mr. SCHAAFF. On April 22, this was the point at which we first notified consumers that there had been an intrusion. We were trying to understand what had happened to the network, and we were actively beginning the investigation of that breach. And at the point that we were able to determine that there had been an intrusion, we immediately notified consumers so that they would be aware of what had occurred, even though at that time we were not yet able to confirm precisely which data may have been compromised.

Mr. BUTTERFIELD. So is it your testimony that on April 22, you began the process of notifying the consumers?

Mr. SCHAAFF. Well, we notified them on the PlayStation blog of the intrusion, but then on April 26, we followed that up with an additional notification regarding more specifics related to the actual data that may have been breached and we began immediately notifying consumers starting from that date via email of the breach as well.

Mr. BUTTERFIELD. But the April 22 announcement was simply on the internet? It was on the blog?

Mr. SCHAAFF. That was posted on the PlayStation blog. The PlayStation blog is one of the most active and popular blogs on the web. It is currently ranked about number 20, just behind the White House blog. So it is a very, very expected place for our consumers to look for information.

Mr. BUTTERFIELD. Do you have any way of knowing how many consumers actually read the statement?

Mr. SCHAAFF. I don't know the answer to that off the top of my head. We can investigate and——

Mr. BUTTERFIELD. But 7 days after the breach was when official notification was issued?

Mr. SCHAAFF. We were not able to determine until the day that we had notified consumers. We were searching for evidence that would allow us to confirm the status of the credit card information and not being able——

Mr. BUTTERFIELD. Do you think 7 days was a reasonable time?

Mr. SCHAAFF. Actually, what has been interesting from my perspective is that we have continued this investigation in the successive weeks, and as you hear me speaking today, some of our conclusions with respect to credit card information have changed somewhat from our original statements. And that change has occurred because of the continuing investigation. In the abundance of caution, we acknowledge the possibility that credit cards would have been taken in our announcements on the 26th. But as you can see, the situation changes as the investigation proceeds, and we felt it would have been irresponsible if we had notified consumers earlier with partial or incomplete information.

Mr. BUTTERFIELD. But you have, based on your experience here, made some corrections and some adjustments in the credit card data that you collect?

Mr. SCHAAFF. We have been working to increase the security of the entire network and additional controls related to credit card data have also been put in place, yes.

Mr. BUTTERFIELD. And how do these measures compare to those for the other types of personal information that you have, the credit card data versus the other information?

Mr. SCHAAFF. Yes, excuse me. The credit card information is the most highly protected and guarded information. It is all encrypted and so even if it is taken, it is not likely to be useful to the hacker.

Mr. BUTTERFIELD. Is it true that user passwords were hashed and not encrypted? Is that true?

Mr. SCHAAFF. That is true. It is true that they were hashed using cryptographic hash functions. That is an industry practice which is very standard. It is not an unusual practice at all.

Mr. BUTTERFIELD. Industry standard. Well, why don't you use any type of encryption in your procedures?

Mr. SCHAAFF. It is a form of protection that is very, very closely related to encryption, and I am not an expert in cryptography so I am not sure that I could answer the question in a more detailed way.

Mr. BUTTERFIELD. What is irreversible encryption?

Mr. SCHAAFF. Irreversible encryption is my understanding of the definition of a cryptographic hash. I am sorry. This is—wait. OK.

Mr. BUTTERFIELD. Ms. Fitzgerald, your testimony states that Epsilon's internal investigation revealed that the login credentials of the employee who reported unusual and suspicious download activity had been compromised. And in layman's terms, I suppose, I assume this means that the employees credentials had been hijacked and been used by a hacker to carry out the intrusion into your network and to steal consumers' email addresses. Can you please tell me a little bit more about what that means, that the employee's login credentials were compromised?

Ms. FITZGERALD. Well, what we had understood during the investigation is that the credentials were somehow used based on the logs, though not necessarily by that person, to actually download that information. That is why we then immediately—our system kicked into place and immediately we saw that there was improper downloads and so our security system kicked in and then we knew that there was a problem and we shut their access down and anybody else who had credentials at that level and took that computer off the system.

Mr. BUTTERFIELD. Thank you. My time has expired.

Mrs. BONO MACK. I thank the gentleman and recognize the gentleman from Florida, Mr. Stearns, for 5 minutes.

Mr. STEARNS. Thank you, Madam Chair. Let me be sure I understand, Ms. Fitzgerald, exactly what was taken. It is our understanding emails were taken and the name of the people whose email was taken. Is that correct?

Ms. FITZGERALD. I am sorry. Was that to me?

Mr. STEARNS. Yes.

Ms. FITZGERALD. I am sorry.

Mr. STEARNS. What was actually taken, as I understand it, is emails——

Ms. FITZGERALD. It was email addresses, and in some cases, first and last names.

Mr. STEARNS. First and last names. OK. And that was all?

Ms. FITZGERALD. Yes.

Mr. STEARNS. And you said that you notified all 50 to 75 customers. Is that correct?

Ms. FITZGERALD. There were about 50 customers of our clients, that were affected.

Mr. STEARNS. OK.

Ms. FITZGERALD. And we notified them.

Mr. STEARNS. Would you provide the committee the complete list of those?

Ms. FITZGERALD. The names of those clients are subject to agreements that we have with them, and we are supposed to keep those confidential.

Mr. STEARNS. So you cannot provide us——

Ms. FITZGERALD. So we notified them promptly so they could——

Mr. STEARNS. No, I know you notified them, but you cannot provide the committee with these names? Is that what you are saying today?

Ms. FITZGERALD. Not at this point, no.

Mr. STEARNS. Now, I have in our material that some of these people are J.P. Morgan Chase, Capital One, Citibank, Best Buy, Verizon, Target, Home Shopping Network, and Verizon. Is that part of the 50 to 75?

Ms. FITZGERALD. I recognize most of those names as being ones that sent us notification——

Mr. STEARNS. They are people that have huge number of people, so the impact of this 50 to 75, we cannot even comprehend how many Verizon has. So can you extrapolate, not telling us in detail, but if Verizon is one of your customers and you had a breach with the emails and names, does that mean that perhaps millions of names from Verizon had been breached?

Ms. FITZGERALD. There could be many.

Mr. STEARNS. Just yes or no.

Ms. FITZGERALD. Yes.

Mr. STEARNS. Yes, oK. Now, with Sony, the question is, as I understand it, the password for the Sony PlayStation was breached. Is that correct?

Mr. SCHAAFF. Well, we believe that there were a number of different types of information accessed, including first name and last name, address, date of birth, login, password, login address——

Mr. STEARNS. For the Sony PlayStation?

Mr. SCHAAFF. For the Sony PlayStation Network, yes.

Mr. STEARNS. OK. And what about their credit cards?

Mr. SCHAAFF. As I said, we had originally stated that there was a possibility. We could not rule out the possibility that the credit card information had been accessed. At this point in time, we do not see any evidence that it has been.

Mr. STEARNS. OK. When you look at the person's credit card together with personal information, his password for Sony PlayStation, would one person have all of that breached for that one person or is it segmented so somebody got their password, somebody got their credit card, somebody got their person or is all this information together when it was breached?

Mr. SCHAAFF. It is difficult for us to know exactly which data was taken, but it is likely that they would have been taken together, but we don't know for which accounts that would have been.

Mr. STEARNS. And what is a conservative estimate the number of people were affected by this breach?

Mr. SCHAAFF. Well, so we have announced that there were approximately 77 million accounts that could have been accessed. When we took the network offline, obviously all of our customers were affected for the period of time that the network has been down, but that is part of the reason why we have provided the identity theft insurance, identity theft protection program, and these welcome back programs was to appreciate and acknowledge the loss of access to the network that our customers experienced and to address the concerns that they may have regarding the loss of their personal information.

Mr. STEARNS. Is it true that you brought suit to protect your IP against the hackers of PlayStation III device?

Mr. SCHAAFF. That is true.

Mr. STEARNS. Why did you bring this suit?

Mr. SCHAAFF. Well, just like the music industry and the movie industry, the PlayStation business is built upon intellectual property. Content providers invest millions of dollars to create titles that we then help them to distribute in our business and the employment of literally tens of thousands of people around the country.

Mr. STEARNS. Knowing what has happened to you with this breach, would you say that you would do it again?

Mr. SCHAAFF. I am sorry. I didn't hear the question.

Mr. STEARNS. Knowing what has happened with this breach, would you go ahead and have done that suit again in hindsight?

Mr. SCHAAFF. Well, I think this is one of the great challenges right now is how do companies protect their content businesses? I mean I think we made the right decision. Did it have consequences? It appears to have had some fairly negative consequences for the company. But if we hadn't done something, I think it would be playing out in a different company later on.

Mr. STEARNS. OK.

Mr. SCHAAFF. I think this is a big issue for the Nation.

Mr. STEARNS. Now, assuming we have federal legislation, do you think federal legislation to address security breaches would help? Because I understand both of you are in States where we have state legislation and that didn't seem to necessarily force you to have a secure data security department. So why would federal legislation make it better than the States who have already passed? And you didn't comply, evidently, with the States.

Mr. SCHAAFF. Well, actually, I think that the issue regarding the States' rights—I am not a lawyer. Let me mention up front I am not a lawyer.

Mr. STEARNS. Right.

Mr. SCHAAFF. But my understanding here is that there are a variety of laws in a number of the States, but the laws are often seemingly in conflict and they can create very complicated situations for us to understand how we should behave properly with regard to notification obligations. Regarding the security of the network, I think the evidence of Epsilon, of Sony, of many other companies that have been reported in the news in the last several weeks indicates that despite spending millions of dollars to secure your networks, despite all of the best methods known to us, our networks are not 100 percent protected. It is a process that requires continual investment, and we do that, but I think without additional support from the government, it is unlikely we will all collectively be successful, and that will threaten the livelihood of the internet, the growing internet economy.

Mr. STEARNS. Thank you.

Mrs. BONO MACK. The gentleman's time has expired. The chair recognizes Mr. Guthrie for 5 minutes.

Mr. GUTHRIE. Thank you, Madam Chairman, for having this hearing. I appreciate it very much.

So just to follow up on what Mr. Stearns said, the patchwork of state laws, the different state jurisdictions complicated your ability to respond? You didn't say that. Is that what I heard?

Mr. SCHAAFF. I was responding specifically to the issue about the notification obligation.

Mr. GUTHRIE. Right, the notification state laws.

Mr. SCHAAFF. It is my understanding that there are some conflicting obligations there.

Mr. GUTHRIE. So a federal standard would be——

Mr. SCHAAFF. A federal standard that would preempt the states would be extremely helpful.

Mr. GUTHRIE. OK. I just want to get kind of the nature—so Epsilon is a vendor for you? Is Epsilon a vendor for Sony? So did the hacker go to Epsilon into Sony or Sony to Epsilon to get to the other—how did that work?

Mr. SCHAAFF. I am sorry. Let me clarify. These are actually two completely separate breach events.

Mr. GUTHRIE. OK.

Mr. SCHAAFF. So the activity at Epsilon was completely unrelated to—as far as we know—what happened at Sony.

Mr. GUTHRIE. So you are not a vendor with Epsilon? This is two completely separate—oK. So the other customers—oK. I was thinking—I apologize. But your other customers, they came—the Epsilon, they got to your system, and then through your system were able to—at least the companies that you notified, the Verizons, the Krogers that was mentioned earlier, that was how that breach worked?

Ms. FITZGERALD. So as a vendor, our ability to send out email addresses on behalf of those clients requires us to maintain those email addresses for them.

Mr. GUTHRIE. Right.

Ms. FITZGERALD. And that is how the hackers got in and got that information.

Mr. GUTHRIE. OK. OK. Has Sony been victim before of any type of breach? And if so, how did that—not to this level, I know, but—
—

Mr. SCHAAFF. We certainly experience a constant level of fraud, and we are under regular probing by hackers and others. I mean I think it is a standard part of anybody who is in the internet business these days.

Mr. GUTHRIE. And for both of you, too, I know I am manufacturing background and we did ISO 9000, which was a set of standards for quality control. They have ISO 14000, a set of standards for environmental—and they are good practices to follow, but they leave a lot of interpretation to the businesses because otherwise they are formed by committee, and it would be difficult to change every time something needs to be changed. I am not familiar with this particular standard that you are talking about, but is it sufficient if you follow the ISO standards to—I guess my question is your industry is so fast-changing that when you are in the automotive industry, which I am in, you put a standard in place, it takes a while for things to innovate that the standard is out of date. It appears to me when I saw ISO that it would be difficult for them to keep up with the changes in the industry or, I guess what I am saying, the ability of people who hack to innovate to find new ways into your system. So is it sufficient—I guess ISO being certified sufficient, you think?

Ms. FITZGERALD. We don't use the ISO as the only thing we do. We have lots of audits by our clients. We have 70 audits we have to do. And then, frankly, we have our own security program where we are continually trying to upgrade our systems and to make sure that we make things as tight as we can, but the hackers are very sophisticated. This wasn't some guy in a garage just coming after us. These are sophisticated guys. And I have talked to the Secret Service enough times now to know that we are not the only one and that they are working with the FBI. And there is a concerted effort to go after these guys.

Mr. SCHAAFF. Um-hum. Yes, I would concur. I mean I think these guidelines and standards are important for the industry to move forward, but they are far from sufficient. And if they had been sufficient, I, you know, I wouldn't be here. And I think that we are all under attack and without additional measures to be taken and without kind of constant renewal of our practices, it is not going to be sufficient to fight the latest attacks.

Mr. GUTHRIE. OK. Thank you. I guess one thing that I am really kind of concerned about as we move forward, I know Sony—any time you spend money because somebody did something illegal, that is an inefficiency to everybody. But the two- or three-store small business in Kentucky that maintains their clients files and just having the resources to be able to respond to protect their clients, to protect their customers. And just do you have any estimate of how much money just these events are going to cost your firm and hits, you know, the economy overall because that is what——

Mr. SCHAAFF. I believe we have made statements publicly estimating a cost something in the range of $170 million for this particular incident. And obviously, as you note, for smaller businesses, number one, the ability to secure their networks as effectively is less because of the economics of that. And the evidence that I have seen in various reports suggest that the prevalence of successful attacks on small and midsize businesses is even higher than we see with the larger companies. It is a scary situation.

Mr. GUTHRIE. Well, thank you. I yield back to the chairwoman.

Mrs. BONO MACK. I thank the gentleman and the chair notes that we are being called to the floor for votes. My intention is to try to get through two more member questioning 5-minute segments before we recess. So the chair now recognizes Mr. Olson for 5 minutes.

Mr. OLSON. I thank the chairwoman. And again, I thank the witnesses for coming and giving us your expertise, your time today.

As I stated in my opening statement, my home State of Texas experienced a serious and troubling data breach earlier this year. Names, addresses, social security numbers, and in some cases, birthdates and drivers' license numbers of state retirees and unemployment beneficiaries were posted unencrypted on a public server. In response, our state attorney general and the FBI have launched a criminal investigation into this data breach. Unfortunately, these kind of breaches are happening more frequently and they cause businesses tens of billions of dollars annually. The Federal Trade Commission estimates that 9 million individuals in the United States have their identities stolen every year. This is the equivalent of approximately 17 identities stolen every minute. That means that during the course of this hearing, if all of my colleagues and I take up our full 5 minutes, 85 IDs across this country will have been stolen.

In response to the Texas data breach, the comptroller of public accounts launched a Web site called Texas Safeguard, which was created as a tool for Texans to receive up-to-date information about the breach, along with recommended security steps to take. And of note, they actually put a toll-free number up for folks to call and the comptroller is offering credit monitoring at no charge. There is also a frequently-asked-questions page which outlines six steps people can take to protect themselves.

But this burden is placed upon these victims of this breach and they have got to spend their own time enrolling in credit monitoring, placing fraud alerts on their credit files, requesting credit reports, and so on, and so on, and so on. Ms. Fitzgerald, Mr. Schaaff, given the breaches your companies have experienced and all the heartache and lost revenue, all the upset customers, all the resources you have had to expend to determine how these breaches occurred, I don't want to put words in your mouth, but you do think that there is a clear need for a comprehensive federal data breach and notification law, one that will create a uniform standard and preempt the current patchwork of state laws? Yea, nay?

Ms. FITZGERALD. I do believe that it would be great if we had a federal data breach notification law that did preempt all of the state laws so it would be straightforward and companies would know exactly what they needed to take care of and who they needed to notify and when they needed to notify?

Mr. OLSON. Mr. Schaaff?

Mr. SCHAAFF. Sony is also very supportive of such legislation and we would be very happy to participate and help in the formation of that legislation.

Mr. OLSON. All right. Thank you. And Ms. Fitzgerald, this is just for you, but why did you choose to contact law enforcement, the FBI, and the Secret Service as soon as you became aware of the incident? And is this a typical response for Epsilon to get law enforcement involved when a breach occurs when you don't necessarily know the extent of it?

Ms. FITZGERALD. Well, we knew pretty quickly that there had been some data that had been downloaded and taken by somebody who wasn't authorized, and therefore, it was a criminal act in our mind. And so we went to look for law enforcement, the right ones to help us go after the bad guys.

Mr. OLSON. OK. And for you, Mr. Schaaff? I know you and PlayStation had one heck of an April. But why did you conclude that notifying PlayStation Network customers via the PlayStation blog was, as you stated, ''one of the best, fastest, and most direct means of communicating with customers?''

Mr. SCHAAFF. In the years that PlayStation has been in business, we have managed this blog and it has become a very, very popular source of information for our customers about new game titles and all kinds of information related to PlayStation. And we know that it is a good way to get a message out to customers quickly. Of course, that wasn't the only way we communicated with our customers. We did follow up with public announcements through other channels, as well as email, direct emails to the consumers following the breach.

Mr. OLSON. OK. And one final question about sort of how you are prepared for this. I mean I know, Ms. Fitzgerald, for your testimony Epsilon had reactive plans in place ready to go if some sort of breach happened, and I assume that is the same for Sony.

Mr. SCHAAFF. Absolutely.

Mr. OLSON. But, I mean, is there a specific entity within both of your companies that is proactive? I mean somebody you have got in your company that sort of looks at your security systems and tries to penetrate it, tries to find the weaknesses; I mean sort of a proactive approach instead of reacting to a breach, preventing a breach by recognizing weaknesses within the company?

Mr. SCHAAFF. We have a successful approach the security involved both proactive as well as reactive approaches, and we definitely have those kinds of resources in place in my company and in Sony Corporation as a whole, an important part of our process.

Ms. FITZGERALD. And I would agree with that also. Epsilon has that.

Mr. OLSON. OK. I see I am down to 16 seconds. I thank the witnesses again for your time. And at the risk of getting crosswise with the chairwoman and Mr. Stearns left, but go Mavericks.

Mr. SCHAAFF. Thank you.

Mrs. BONO MACK. The chair recognizes Mr. Harper for 5 minutes.

Mr. HARPER. Thank you, Madam Chair. I would ask you, Mr. Schaaff, why did it take Sony approximately 7 days to notify customers that their personal data had been compromised?

Mr. SCHAAFF. Well, the basic essence here was the find the right balance between notifying customers as soon as we had some sense that something had gone wrong but not being irresponsible in that notification and creating undue stress or concern within the customer base. We immediately began an investigation and we were able to notify customers within a couple of days that we had had an unauthorized external intrusion. But it took us several more days to be able to clearly discern what information had been taken and even at that point, we were not able to rule out the possibility that credit card information had been taken. Nevertheless, we went ahead and made a public statement regarding the potential of those losses.

Mr. HARPER. I just want to be clear. So how long was it before any customers got notification?

Mr. SCHAAFF. We first discovered unusual activity on the 19th. We shut down the network on the 20th of April, and we notified consumers on the 22nd of April. So it was basically 2 days.

Mr. HARPER. Did you notify all the consumers at that point?

Mr. SCHAAFF. Well, so at that point we were intensely involved in this investigation to try to figure out what to notify the customers about. And so at that time we notifying using the blog that we believed that there had been an intrusion. And then beginning on the 26th when we made a lot of public announcements related to specific information that may have been lose we initiated through news channels, obviously our blog, as well as through a direct email campaign to the customers detailed information about the nature of the loss.

Mr. HARPER. How many notifications did each consumer receive?

Mr. SCHAAFF. Well, my understanding is that in regard to the Sony PlayStation breach, that should have been approximately 77 million emails that were sent.

Mr. HARPER. Now, I understand but were they notified more than one time as you learned additional information?

Mr. SCHAAFF. Well, we notified via the blog on the 22nd. We provide updates on that blog on a regular basis as to kind of the concurrent state of affairs, but I believe in terms of the email notifications related to the potential loss of data, that was a one-time event.

Mr. HARPER. Do you believe the news that you passed on, looking back now, do you believe it was done quickly enough?

Mr. SCHAAFF. What I would say is that we tried very, very hard to find the right balance there, and I believe that if we had responded earlier, it would have probably been irresponsible. Even to this day we question whether we should have taken a little bit more time to finish the investigation with regard to the credit card information. I believe we probably struck the right balance, but it was a tough call.

Mr. HARPER. And I know there was a letter that was sent out on May 3 where you had indicated that there was no evidence of misuse of the customers' personal information that was accessed during that breach. We are a month past that point. Is that still your position on that?

Mr. SCHAAFF. When we talked to the credit card companies, they have still told us that they see no signs of unusual activity related to this breach.

Mr. HARPER. And do you know where the attacks originated?

Mr. SCHAAFF. Unfortunately, at this time we don't.

Mr. HARPER. OK.

Mr. SCHAAFF. We are working with law enforcement and others to try to figure that out, but at this time we don't have any clear——

Mr. HARPER. Of course, we certainly hear media reports or speculation, and I know you don't have it with any certainty, but there was one report that initially suggested that Amazon's pay-per-use cloud service may have been used. Is there any accuracy to that or any proof of that?

Mr. SCHAAFF. Well, so what I know is the FBI is investigating that report, and at this time I don't have any other information about whether that is true or not.

Mr. HARPER. Now, does Sony Online Entertainment and Sony Network Entertainment, are they using the same server models and security protections and the software?

Mr. SCHAAFF. We comply with the same types of industry practices and are subject to the same policies as far as being a part of the Sony Corporation. The specific architecture of each of those services is probably different because the types of services that we provide are different. But, you know, across the industry, most internet service providers are building their services out of largely the same basic components so there is probably a lot of commonality there.

Mr. HARPER. Thank you. Madam Chair, I yield back the balance of my time.

Mrs. BONO MACK. I thank the gentleman. And at this point in time we are going to recess the committee to head over to the floor for vote. And our intention is to return as soon after as we can from the series of votes. It should be about 45 minutes is my guess. Things could change. So the subcommittee stands recessed until after the last vote on the floor.

Ms. FITZGERALD. Thank you.

[Recess.]

Mrs. BONO MACK. The subcommittee will reconvene and come to order obviously. I wanted to thank you very much for indulging us and apologize that there has been a slight little change of plans with the minority headed over to the White House for a very important meeting with the President. We have agreed that we would conclude questions.

But before I do that, I would like to offer the two of you the opportunity to give us any final thoughts you might have and any recommendations for legislation as we move forward in the process here. So I recognize each of you for 5 minutes to do that. And you don't have to take the full 5 minutes if you would like, but the time is yours if you would like it.

Ms. FITZGERALD. Thank you. Honestly, as we have thought about this, we would greatly appreciate the opportunity to work with you and your staff and any members of your subcommittee to create a national data breach notification standard. The details within it would have to be worked out as we think through what would be all the ramifications. And I think clearly I would not be the only one with experience, but we would love to work with that on you.

Mrs. BONO MACK. Mr. Schaaff?

Mr. SCHAAFF. Thank you. I want to thank you again for the opportunity to come and speak today and especially thank you for all the work you have done related to intellectual property protection. This is a really critical part of the work we are trying to do to build and grow our business.

As you heard in our testimony today and in the private session where we shared more technical details regarding the breach yesterday, despite taking what we believe to be extremely appropriate and substantial steps to build a safe and protected network, hackers were able to get into the network. The thing that is frightening about this is it is easy to focus on Sony and look at the things that we might be able to do in the future to strengthen our network, but the reality is because we are all building our networks out of the same basic ingredients, if there is a weakness in the way that we have built things, chances are, the weaknesses may lie in the components that we rely on from the variety of vendors that we all build our products out of. And I think that we are working together as industry to try to strengthen our processes and our practices and our technologies, but I think the conclusion that I would leave you with today is that without further assistance from the government, I think that we are all going to have a world of hurt in this internet economy. And we really would appreciate and request your assistance.

And regarding the specific legislation, we are also extremely supportive of this and would welcome the opportunity to contribute and speak to you further regarding its development. Thank you.

Mrs. BONO MACK. Well, I thank you both very much. And Mr. Schaaff, I would also like to address a comment earlier about the question of would you or would you not file suit again to protect your intellectual property, and I wanted to commend you on your answer. And I am glad that you did it then. And you know, too often people are afraid of being hacked and the retribution because of the decisions you make.

Mr. SCHAAFF. It can be a lonely place.

Mrs. BONO MACK. Well, I want to applaud you for that. And again, thank you both very much for the spirit with which you came before us today and the spirit of cooperation. I think the committee is very excited about the opportunity to work with you and to craft good legislation.

So we have a unique opportunity now as a subcommittee to make certain that the future cyber attacks on American consumers will never again be a silent crime.

So at this point I would like to remind all members they have 10 business days to submit questions for the record, and I ask witnesses to please respond promptly to any questions they receive. And the hearing is now adjourned.

Mr. SCHAAFF. Thank you very much.

Ms. FITZGERALD. Thank you very much.

[Whereupon, at 2:14 p.m., the subcommittee was adjourned.]

[Material submitted for inclusion in the record follows:]

PREPARED STATEMENT OF HON. HENRY A. WAXMAN

I would like to thank Chairman Bono Mack and Ranking Member Butterfield for following this important issue. Data security is not a partisan issue. It is an issue that affects all of us because sooner or later everyone is vulnerable to cyber attacks: private sector companies of all sizes; federal, state and local governments; and the American public.

Just yesterday, we learned of an attempted attack on Google email accounts that included efforts to steal email passwords and other information from high-ranking government and military officials—a stark reminder of the financial and national security risks posed by hackers.

At last month's hearing titled "The Threat of Data Theft to American Consumers," we reviewed how the federal government investigates data breaches and what it should do to ensure that private sector companies protect the personal information of their consumers.

Today we are going to hear from Sony and Epsilon, two companies that recently suffered massive data breaches.

We have all heard the numbers: the personal information in over 100 million user accounts was compromised in the Sony breach. The customers of more than 50 major corporations were affected by the Epsilon breach, including customers of Target, Best Buy, JP Morgan, and US Bank.

While we will delve into the specifics of these two breaches, the point isn't to make an example of these two companies. We need to know how these breaches happened and to find out what these companies are doing, and what they can do better. And we need to understand the appropriate federal role in this area. We need a government that can partner with companies to make sure they do a better job protecting the information they demand of consumers.

As I said at the last hearing, the private sector can, and must, safeguard personal information. If companies do not take reasonable steps to guard their data and they suffer a cyber attack or data breach, the cost to consumers can be immense.

When it comes to data security, prevention is the best medicine and certainly the cheapest. Yet too many companies are not doing enough prevention and consumers are paying the price.

We in Congress also have a role; we can conduct oversight and legislate when needed. The recent attacks on Sony, Epsilon, and now Gmail are proof that it is indeed time to legislate. In particular, Congress should pass the Data Accountability and Trust Act; H.R. 2221 from the 111th Congress.

The bill requires companies to have reasonable data security measures in place and to notify consumers once a breach has occurred. It passed the House last Congress with strong support from both sides of the aisle. We should take swift action to pass it in this Congress.

I look forward to today's hearing and working together to ensure that the private sector is doing all that it can to protect the personal information of the American people.

PREPARED STATEMENT OF HON. EDOLPHUS TOWNS

Thank you Chairman Bono-Mack and Ranking Member Butterfield for holding this hearing today on the importance of Data Security to our nation. The information age has ushered in a new era in technology that offers many Americans the ability to access, store and transfer massive amounts of information at any given time. With the advent of the internet and the advancement of e-commerce, Americans have been able to engage in a variety of online activities that require personal information to be shared in cyber space.

Unfortunately more often than not this information is compromised by computer savvy individuals that use this information to access the identity of their victims. Data breaches have become more common in recent years due to the massive amounts of personal information that are stored on computer servers which many people thought were secure. In April of this year Sony Corporation and Epsilon Data Management revealed they had been involved in two of the biggest data breaches this year. Sony made public that its Play Station Network had been breached on April 26th, 2011; however the breach took place one week prior to their notification of Play Station account holders. The Sony Play Station Network has over 77 million accounts that were compromised due to this lapse in security. It is my hope that this hearing will shed light on how this breach was able to take place and why it took a week for Sony to notify its account holders.

Epsilon Data Management LLC is one of the largest email marketing companies in the country. Over 40 billion emails are sent from this company annually to consumers. On April 1, 2011 Epsilon revealed that an unauthorized entry to its email system had occurred, exposing the personal information of several million customers of companies employing Epsilon for marketing purposes. Reportedly consumer information had been available for months.

Consumers must feel safe in knowing that the information that they share with companies involved in e-commerce is safe and secure. The recent data breaches at the Sony Corporation and Epsilon Data Management raise questions about what protocols are in place to protect consumers against hackers who would do them harm. Currently there is no comprehensive federal law that requires all companies that hold consumer's personal information to implement reasonable measures to protect that data.

I look forward to working with my colleagues on this committee to ensure the American people that their personal information is kept safe from malicious cyber attacks.

Thank you madam chair, I yield my time.

---

epsilon.

July 11, 2011

Chairman Mary Bono Mack	Ranking Member G.K. Butterfield
Subcommittee on Commerce,	Subcommittee on Commerce,
Manufacturing & Trade	Manufacturing & Trade
House Committee on Energy & Commerce	House Committee on Energy & Commerce
U.S. House of Representatives	U.S. House of Representatives
2125 Rayburn House Office Building	2322A Rayburn House Office Building
Washington, D.C. 20515	Washington, D.C. 20515

Dear Chairman Bono Mack and Ranking Member Butterfield:

I am writing on behalf of Epsilon Data Management LLC ("Epsilon") in response to your June 29th correspondence requesting Epsilon's answers to additional questions posed by Representative Dingell. We hope that our attached responses help supplement the record following my June 2nd testimony before the Subcommittee.

Please let us know if we can be of further assistance.

Sincerely,
Epsilon Data Management, LLC

Jeanette Fitzgerald
SVP and General Counsel

cc: The Honorable Fred Upton, Chairman
The Honorable Henry A. Waxman, Ranking Member

AllianceData™

7500 Dallas Parkway
Suite 700
Plano, TX 75024
214-494-3000
108619-v3

Loyalty and Marketing
Services

www.epsilon.com

epsilon.

Responses to Questions from The Honorable John D. Dingell

1. **Do you believe current industry efforts with respect to ensuring data security are sufficient?**

It is difficult for Epsilon to evaluate and comment on how other companies ensure data security. We are prepared, however, to provide Epsilon's perspective on our continuing efforts to ensure that we maintain and implement a state-of-the-art data security program.

Epsilon has always sought to maintain an information security program conforming to the highest standards. As the March intrusion into our e-mail services platform made clear, however, no company, no matter how rigorous its security policies and practices, can ensure that hackers intent on stealing information will not break into its data systems. Epsilon understands how important it is for us to continue to enhance our security policies and procedures to stay ahead of the hackers. Thus, immediately following the March intrusion we took steps to contain the impact of that intrusion, and since then we have worked with experts in the data security field to further improve our practices. By doing so, we believe we are doing what is necessary to help stay on top of data security threats. We also believe that industry cooperation with law enforcement is a key facet to ensuring data security. Companies should not be hesitant to bring in law enforcement as soon as possible following an intrusion. Through cooperation with law enforcement, industry can help ensure that the criminal elements behind these attacks are brought to justice, and consumer information is protected.

2. **Do you believe the Congress should pass comprehensive data security legislation?**

Yes, Epsilon fully supports national legislation that would create a uniform standard for data security and breach notification.

3. **Comprehensive data security requirements do not exist in the United States. Rather, there exists a patchwork of federal and state laws and regulations that impose varying requirements on entities. Should federal data security requirements supersede state requirements? Further, should state attorneys-general be allowed to enforce federal data security requirements?**

Epsilon agrees that the current patchwork of individual state breach notification laws only serves to create confusion among consumers and businesses, and imposes unnecessary compliance costs. A uniform national law, on the other hand, would provide predictability and equity for consumers, regardless of their state of residence, and would make it much easier and less costly for business to ensure any applicable notification requirements are met. A national law, however, can only be successful in eliminating the current unnecessary patchwork of state laws if federal requirements supersede state requirements. As long as federal law sets uniform

AllianceData™

7500 Dallas Parkway
Suite 700
Plano, TX 75024
214-494-3000
108619-v3

Loyalty and Marketing
Services

www.epsilon.com

epsilon.

standards, enforcement by state attorneys general could have the positive effect of putting more "cops on the beat" in the fight against unlawful data intrusions.

4. **Do you believe federal data security legislation should include the flexibility for the Federal Trade Commission to update requirements in order to keep pace with advancements in threats to data security?**

Epsilon believes the FTC is playing an important role regarding data security, and should continue to do so. Further, we believe Congress should ensure that both the Commission and the industry retain the greatest flexibility by enacting a law that is technologically neutral. In that way, the FTC and companies will be in the best position to evaluate security needs as technology evolves, keep pace with new methodologies to protect data, and stay on top of new tactics used by hackers intent on breaking into data systems. Any requirements promulgated by legislation or subsequently through rulemaking by the FTC must be sufficiently flexible to allow businesses to adapt their security procedures to account for the sensitivity of the data they collect, store, or process, and the level of risk involved.

5. **Do you believe the FTC's cumbersome Magnusson-Moss rulemaking procedures would stifle the Commission's ability to write rules that keep pace with technological advancements in threats to data security? If so, do you believe the FTC should be allowed to write data security regulations according to the Administrative Procedure Act, which — while still thorough — is a more expeditious process than Magnusson-Moss?**

While I understand that the Magnusson-Moss rulemaking procedures include additional requirements over the Administrative Procedure Act, unfortunately I do not believe I am qualified to speak as to the import of the FTC using one form of rulemaking procedure over the other.

6. **Further, I ask that both witnesses comment for the record on the reasonableness, appropriateness, and practicability of requiring in law that entities which hold personal data provide customers with some form of insurance to mitigate potential damages caused to them by data breaches.**

Insurance in the form of credit monitoring may be reasonable and appropriate where there is a substantial risk of identity theft resulting from a data breach. Credit monitoring is not practical or necessary, however, where there is not a substantial risk of identity theft.

 AllianceData™

Loyalty and Marketing
Services

www.epsilon.com

7500 Dallas Parkway
Suite 700
Plano, TX 75024
214-494-3000
108619-v3

FRED UPTON, MICHIGAN
CHAIRMAN

HENRY A. WAXMAN, CALIFORNIA
RANKING MEMBER

ONE HUNDRED TWELFTH CONGRESS

Congress of the United States

House of Representatives

COMMITTEE ON ENERGY AND COMMERCE
2125 RAYBURN HOUSE OFFICE BUILDING
WASHINGTON, DC 20515–6115

Majority (202) 225–2927
Minority (202) 226–3641

June 29, 2011

Mr. Tim Schaaff
President
Sony Network Entertainment International
919 East Hillside Boulevard
Forster City, CA 94404

Dear Mr. Schaaff:

Thank you for appearing before the Subcommittee on Commerce, Manufacturing, and Trade on Thursday, June 2, 2011, to testify at the hearing entitled "Sony and Epsilon: Lessons for Data Security Legislation."

Pursuant to the Rules of the Committee on Energy and Commerce, the hearing record remains open for 10 business days to permit Members to submit additional questions to witnesses, which are attached. The format of your responses to these questions should be as follows: (1) the name of the Member whose question you are addressing, (2) the complete text of the question you are addressing in bold, and then (3) your answer to that question in plain text.

To facilitate the printing of the hearing record, please respond to these questions by the close of business on Thursday, July 14, 2011. Your responses should be e-mailed to the Legislative Clerk, in Word or PDF format, at Allison.Busbee@mail.house.gov.

Thank you again for your time and effort preparing and delivering testimony before the Subcommittee.

Sincerely,

Mary Bono Mack
Mary Bono Mack
Chairman
Subcommittee on Commerce, Manufacturing, and Trade

cc: G.K. Butterfield, Ranking Member,
Subcommittee on Commerce, Manufacturing, and Trade

Attachment

SONY

Sony Network Entertainment
989 East Hillsdale Boulevard, Foster City, California 94404

July 21, 2011

The Honorable Mary Bono Mack
Chairman
Subcommittee on Commerce, Manufacturing and Trade
United States Congress
2125 Rayburn House Office Building
Washington D.C. 20515

The Honorable G.K. Butterfield
Ranking Member
Subcommittee on Commerce, Manufacturing and Trade
United States Congress
2125 Rayburn House Office Building
Washington D.C. 20515

Dear Chairman Bono Mack and Ranking Member Butterfield:

Thank you for allowing me to appear before the Subcommittee on Commerce, Manufacturing
and Trade on Thursday June 2, 2011 at the hearing "Sony and Epsilon: Lessons for Data
Security Legislation." This letter is in response to your request for a response to Additional
Questions for the Record by members of the Committee. Some of the references to "Sony" in
the questions do not specify which company is meant. For clarity, unless otherwise indicated, I
will refer to my company, Sony Network Entertainment America Inc., as "SNEA" and, when
referring to other Sony companies or Sony Corporation as a whole, I will specifically identify
those companies by their proper names.

In response to the Committee's questions from:

The Honorable G.K. Butterfield:

1.   In a briefing with Committee staff prior to the hearing, you indicated that Sony's
internal investigation had not discovered any evidence suggesting that credit card data was
taken from the network. This does not necessarily mean this data was not taken, merely
that Sony has not, to date, turned up any digital fingerprints that would allow the company
to know with certainty whether credit card information was exposed.

   a.   Is it still the case today that Sony has not discovered any evidence suggesting
that credit card data was taken?

      Yes, it remains the case today that there is no evidence credit card data was accessed or
      taken. In addition, the credit card brands continue to report that there has been no
      increase in fraudulent transactions as a result of the intrusion.

Letter to Honorable Mary Bono Mack &
Honorable G. K. Butterfield
July 21, 2011
Page 2 of 16

    b.   **Is your internal investigation complete and if not, when will it be completed?**

The internal investigation of the scope of the intrusion, which is being overseen by SNEA's counsel, is still underway. We are not certain when it will be completed.

2.   **Sony began informing its customers that their credit card information might have been exposed about one week after the breach occurred.**

    a.   **Can you explain what was happening that week? For example, was that when you determined you were not going to be able to discover evidence that credit card data was taken?**

As explained in the prior responses by SNEA's affiliate, Sony Computer Entertainment America LLC, to Questions from the Subcommittee on Commerce, Manufacturing and Trade, during the days that followed discovery of the intrusion, SNEA was investigating the scope of the intrusion and what the intruder might have accessed or taken. SNEA elected to inform customers when it believed it understood the potential scope of the intrusion. At that time, although it had no evidence that credit card data had been accessed or taken, SNEA believed it would not immediately be able to rule that out. Had SNEA taken more time to investigate, it might have been able to advise customers that it was very unlikely that credit or payment card data had been taken, but that would have required significantly more time.

    b.   **Do you believe this was a reasonable time frame for providing notice to customers? Why or why not?**

SNEA believes that its timing was entirely reasonable. SNEA began notifying its customers within a week of discovering the intrusion. The decision to notify customers was made during a period of uncertainty. SNEA had to balance what it believed it knew against information that was unconfirmed, while at the same time trying to preserve and protect evidence, and make appropriate business decisions related to the operation of its network. Given more time, SNEA may have been able to provide more assurances to customers that their payment card information had not been accessed. At the time, however, SNEA felt it was better to provide the details of what it believed may have been accessed so that customers were informed. Indeed, SNEA appears to have responded considerably faster than many other companies that found themselves in similar situations—so SNEA strongly believes that it acted in a reasonable time frame.

3.   **What measures did Sony take to protect credit card information prior to the cyberattack? How do these measures compare to those for other types of personal information you maintain? Within the realm of options known to you for securing credit card information, how do your methods compare to other options?**

Access to data on the SNEA network was restricted through the perimeter firewalls and security systems in its network. SNEA's procedure was to encrypt payment card

Letter to Honorable Mary Bono Mack &
Honorable G. K. Butterfield
July 21, 2011
Page 3 of 16

information, and to protect user passwords by a cryptographic hash. Within the realm of options known for securing credit card information, we believe that SNEA methods are comparable to industry norms.

4. **Sony's May 3 letter in response to written questions from this Committee states several possible reasons that the Sony Network Entertainment America team did not detect the intrusion into its network infrastructure. Among those possible reasons is that SNEA's security teams had turned their attention to defending against denial-of-service attacks orchestrated by the group known as Anonymous.**

Sony's letter goes on to state the following: "Whether those who participated in the denial of services attacks were conspirators or whether they were simply duped into providing cover for a very clever thief, we may never know. In any case, those who participated in the denial of service attacks should understand that—whether they knew it or not—they were aiding in a well planned, well executed, large-scale theft that left not only Sony a victim, but also Sony's many customers around the world"

Sony's May 26 letter in response to written questions from this panel seems more measured in drawing a connection between the denial-of-service attacks and the network intrusion that occurred around the same time. That letter states: "We now know that at some time during or shortly after those [denial-of-service] attacks, one or more highly skilled hackers infiltrated the servers of SNEA and SOE"

The first letter suggests that Sony strongly believed that the denial-of-service attacks were orchestrated to provide cover for the network intrusion. However, the second letter seems to suggest they were only closely related in time, but not necessarily jointly, orchestrated.

   a. **Please clarify: What is Sony's current understanding of the relationship between the denial-of-service attacks and the larger network intrusion?**

   The network intrusion occurred during the period that denial-of-service attacks took place. Anonymous claimed responsibility for the denial-of-service attacks and other threats but subsequently disclaimed responsibility for any theft of customer information. Anonymous conceded, however, that the person who was responsible for the intrusion could have been an Anonymous member. SNEA has not identified the person or persons responsible for the network intrusion and therefore does not know if the attacks and intrusion were jointly orchestrated to take place concurrently, or if the intruder attempted to use the denial-of-service attacks as an opportunity to cover access to SNEA's system, or otherwise.

   b. **Was the company on guard for any other types of potential attacks around this time? If so, please explain what other attacks you anticipated and how you prepared for those other types of attacks. If not, why not?**

Letter to Honorable Mary Bono Mack &
Honorable G. K. Butterfield
July 21, 2011
Page 4 of 16

SNEA was on guard for other potential attacks at the time of the denial-of-service attacks, both in accordance with its overall information security program and, in particular, as a result of Anonymous threats. SNEA had prepared for other types of attacks by putting in place the robust information security system that protected its network, which included, for example, that access to data on the network was restricted, both credit card and personal data were behind a sophisticated security system, and user password information was transformed using a cryptographic hash function.

5.   In the company's May 3 response to written questions from this Committee, Sony laid out briefly the sequence of events leading up to the decision to completely shut down all PlayStation Network services.

According to that letter, On the evening of April 19, the network team at Sony Network, Entertainment America (SNEA) discovered that several "servers unexpectedly rebooted themselves and that unplanned unusual activity was taking place on the network." At this point, the team took four servers offline and began an internal assessment.

On the afternoon of April 20, the network team discovered evidence suggesting an unauthorized intrusion had occurred and that data had been transferred off PlayStation Network servers without authorization. At this point, the team discovered that six more servers, or 10 total, had possibly been compromised. The team could not at that time determine what type of data had been transferred and the entire PlayStation Network was shut down.

Just before the time of this breach, Sony was also the target of denial-of-service attacks, and hired an outside firm in early April to help it fend off these attacks.

a.   Was the team that discovered the intrusion involved with defending against the denial-of-service attacks that occurred around the time of the hack? Can you please describe their involvement?

Yes, the team that was involved in defending against the denial-of-service attacks included individuals who detected the unusual activity that led to the discovery of the intrusion.

b.   If this team was not involved with defending against the denial-of-service attacks, to what extent would this team have been aware that Sony was being targeted for such attacks? On what other network security activities would this team have been focused during the month of April?

The network security team was responsible for all aspects of network security during the month of April. The team's focus in April was on the denial-of-service attacks and the intrusion. Prior to the attacks, the security team was also preparing to move the network's operations to its new facilities and, through the month of April, those preparations continued to move forward as well.

Letter to Honorable Mary Bono Mack &
Honorable G. K. Butterfield
July 21, 2011
Page 5 of 16

6.   **In the briefing with Committee staff prior to the hearing at which you testified, you stated that you made the decision to completely shut down the PlayStation Network on April 20.**

    a.   **Can you please explain how and why you made the decision to shut down the PlayStation Network? What factors contributed to your decision to take this significant step? Was this an impromptu decision? Were there policies or procedures in place that required that the network be shut down under these circumstances? If so, can you please describe the substance of those policies or procedures?**

    When the security team discovered that there had been an intrusion, that information was reported up to SNEA executive management, which was consistent with relevant policies. The decision to shut down was made because it was clear that the system had been intruded upon and an investigation was necessary to determine the scope of the intrusion. The factors that went into the decision were the potential risks to customers, the potential risk to SNEA's business, concern that the hackers would take control or deface the site and the need to prevent further unauthorized access. The decision to shut down the network was made quickly but was not an impromptu decision.

    b.   **Was anyone else involved with making this decision? Please list each person who was involved with or consulted about this decision.**

    The decision was made by myself and the executive management for my company based on information provided by the security team and after advising Sony Corporation senior management.

7.   **Sony's May 3 letter to this panel states that the Sony Network Entertainment America (SNEA) team did not immediately detect the criminal intrusion. The letter goes on to list three possible reasons. The second reason listed is: "[D]etection was difficult because the criminal hackers exploited a system software vulnerability."**

    a.   **Please explain what the company meant when it wrote that the "hackers exploited a system software vulnerability"?**

    The letter was referencing an exploitable feature that existed in software on system servers that the intruder was able to exploit.

    b.   **Was this system software vulnerability known to Sony prior to the cyberattack? If so, why had nothing been done prior to the attack to deal with this software vulnerability?**

    SNEA's investigation of circumstances surrounding the exploitable feature of the software remains underway.

Letter to Honorable Mary Bono Mack &
Honorable G. K. Butterfield
July 21, 2011
Page 6 of 16

  c. What steps have you taken to protect against this vulnerability?

The software settings have been reconfigured.

  d. What steps are you taking to detect and minimize other system software vulnerabilities?

Steps SNEA is taking to detect and minimize software vulnerabilities include, for example, automatic detection of up-to-date system patching information, monthly external and internal vulnerability scans, comprehensive penetration testing, and regular review of relevant industry resources.

8. Sony has offered its U.S. customers a one year, $1 million identify theft insurance policy. Please explain how this sort of protection works and how customers sign up for this service.

SNEA has made arrangements with Debix, Inc., one of the industry's most reputable identity protection firms, to offer the AllClear ID PLUS identity theft protection program to eligible customers who are concerned about identity theft.

AllClear ID PLUS includes:

- Cyber monitoring and surveillance of the Internet to detect exposure of an AllClear ID Plus customer's personal information, including monitoring of criminal web sites and data recovered by law enforcement. If his/her personal information is found, the customer will be alerted by phone and/or email and will be provided advice and support regarding protective steps to take. The customer will also receive monthly identity status reports. Debix works with an alliance of cyber-crime experts from the government, academia and industry to provide these services.

- Priority access to licensed private investigators and identity restoration specialists. If an AllClear ID Plus customer receives an alert, or otherwise suspects that he/she may be the victim of identity theft, the customer can speak directly, on a priority basis, with an on-staff licensed private investigator, who will conduct a comprehensive inquiry. In the case of an identity theft, the customer can work with an identity restoration specialist to restore his/her identity. The restoration specialist would contact creditors and others, and take necessary steps to restore the customer's identity.

- A $1 million identity theft insurance policy per user to provide additional protection in the event that an AllClear ID Plus customer becomes a victim of identity theft. This insurance would provide financial relief of up to $1 million for covered identity restoration costs, legal defense expenses, and lost wages that occur within 12 months after the stolen identity event.

All customers have been sent e-mails offering the service and eligible customers have until July 31, 2011 to sign up, which they may do via the internet.

Letter to Honorable Mary Bono Mack &
Honorable G. K. Butterfield
July 21, 2011
Page 7 of 16

9.   Sony has not offered customers credit monitoring services or offered to provide for credit freezes. New York Times business columnist Ron Lieber took particular issue with Sony's failure to offer the credit freeze service. Lieber wrote: "Credit freezes are the best defense mechanism available for people whose data may have fallen into the wrong hands, and it's a shame that Sony executives don't seem to have realized this." Regarding the freeze service, Lieber wrote: "Once you put your credit reports on ice at the three major credit bureaus . . . no company (other than ones you already do business with) can look at your credit report. Creditors generally won't open a new account if they don't have access to the report, so a freeze offers the best protection there is against someone opening an account in your name."

     a.   Please explain why Sony has not offered to pay for customers to freeze their credit reports.

          Currently no evidence exists that payment card information was taken, and all available evidence suggests that it was not taken. In addition, the major credit card companies continue to advise SNEA that there has been no increase in fraudulent transactions resulting from this breach. Finally, as is reflected in most if not all proposed federal legislation, credit monitoring may be appropriate when certain kinds of data are taken, but SNEA does not collect such data. A freeze on credit reports does not appear warranted given these circumstances.

     b.   Please explain why Sony has not offered credit monitoring services.

          For the reasons identified above, at this time credit monitoring services do not appear to be warranted.

10.   Sony's May 3 letter in response to written questions from this Committee states that among the new security measures taken following the breach is the naming of a new Chief Information Security Officer reporting directly to Sony Corporation's Chief Information Officer.

     a.   Please clarify which company named a new Chief Information Security Officer: Sony Network Entertainment America? Sony Online Entertainment? Sony Corporation?

          Sony Network Entertainment International LLC established the new position of Chief Information Security Officer.

     b.   Is this a new position, a personnel change, or did you fill a vacancy? Is this a permanent appointment?

          This is a new position, senior to the existing IT security team at Sony Network Entertainment International LLC and with reporting lines that include Sony Corporation. The position is permanent.

c. **Please describe what responsibilities this person will take on?**

The Chief Information Security Officer will be responsible for the overall strategy and execution for establishing and maintaining an enterprise-wide information security program to ensure that all information access globally for Sony Network Entertainment is adequately protected. Responsibilities will include identifying, evaluating and reporting on information security risks in a manner that meets both compliance and regulatory requirements while staying ahead of all information security risks and exposures, as well as carrying out various component elements of those programs. The Chief Information Security Officer will also be responsible to establish a technology protection and continuity capability including physical and environmental security, continuity planning and system integrity.

d. **Why was no one serving in this role prior to the breach?**

Prior to the breach, Sony Network Entertainment International LLC had its own IT Security Officer and security team. Those individuals will continue in their positions, reporting into the new Chief Security Information Officer, who will oversee and coordinate issues related to securing information.

11. **Soon after news of the cyber attacks became public, Seth Schlessel wrote in the New York Times that: "The root issue is that Sony has never made the transition from an electronics and media company focused on physical products to a software and services company focused on providing experiences. And now it is paying a huge price in its online credibility and reputation." He continued, posing the following question: "Once Sony inevitably assures us that everything is fine, who, exactly, is going to volunteer to trust the company again with personal financial information?"**

a. **Can Sony assure its customers that they can trust Sony with their personal financial information?**

SNEA limited its collection of financial data to payment card information and does not collect other personal financial information. SNEA's procedure was to encrypt this information, and we believe it was never accessed. In response to this intrusion SNEA has increased its network security so SNEA believes that its customers can feel assured that SNEA has taken and is taking appropriate steps to protect financial information that they provide SNEA.

b. **What has Sony done to back up any assurances to its customers that it will do a better job of protecting their data?**

SNEA has increased security, moved its network operations to a new facility, heightened IT security awareness in the company, and communicated directly with its customers about the breach. As noted, a new Chief Information Security Officer position has been created as well.

Letter to Honorable Mary Bono Mack &
Honorable G. K. Butterfield
July 21, 2011
Page 9 of 16

12.   In order to understand more about the breaches affecting your U.S. customers, the Committee has written two letters and met with Sony staff on three separate occasions. Several times, in response, the company provided incomplete information. Sony did eventually provide the Committee with a confidential technical briefing that proved helpful. But some questions remain.

    a.   Has Sony now identified all the information residing on the servers that were compromised, and can you say with certainty that you understand the extent of the breach?

    SNEA has been able to identify the information that was residing on the customer database that was accessed and believes that it has developed a strong understanding of the extent of the breach. SNEA feels comfortable it has notified customers of the type of information about them that the intruder may have accessed or taken.

13.   Since the initial breach, several other Sony companies have made public that breaches of their networks have occurred. Does Sony Corporation have any company-wide information security policies and procedures? If so, how have those security policies and procedures changes as a result of the continued attacks on Sony networks?

    Sony Corporation utilizes a global framework for providing policies to its group companies to ensure consistent standard information security practices for each operating company. The Global Information Security Policy ("GISP") sets forth the company's information security management structure and administrative, technical and physical safeguards to protect the confidentiality, integrity, and availability of non-public information. The GISP also defines the overall direction and policy of Sony Group's information security program and the authorities and responsibilities for information security management. Additionally, Sony Corporation provides a set of 14 standards, Global Information Security Standards ("GISS"), that specify the types of controls needed for the different categories of information security management (e.g., information classification, access controls and HR security).

    Sony Corporation has undertaken a global initiative to review information security policies, standards and procedures to identify areas that should be strengthened given the realities of an environment with an increasing threat of hacking and illegal intrusions.

14.   Sony was warned earlier this year that it would be the target of denial-of-service attacks in retaliation for legal action against a hacker that broke some of the code protecting the PlayStation 3 console. Sony hired a team from the security firm Prolexic to help the company protect its network after the denial-of-service attacks began.

    a.   When did Sony become aware of the risk of denial-of-service attacks?

    SNEA became aware of the risk it would be a target of denial-of-service attacks on March 10, 2011.

Letter to Honorable Mary Bono Mack &
Honorable G. K. Butterfield
July 21, 2011
Page 10 of 16

b.   **On what date did the denial-of-service attacks begin?**

The denial-of-service attacks began on or around March 10, 2011, but IT security of the affected Sony Corporation companies was able to defend against the early attacks. On April 3, 2011, Anonymous publically announced its "opsSony" plan to attack Sony Corporation companies resulting in a spike in the attacks over the following link: **http://anonops.blogspot.com/2011/04/opsony.html**. In response to the increasing intensity of the denial-of-service attacks, SNEA felt it was necessary to seek assistance and engaged Prolexic.

c.   **On what date did Sony hire Prolexic?**

On or about April 4th.

d.   **It seems that Sony was aware of the risk of a specific cyber-attack before the attack commenced and chose to take steps to deal with the attack only after it began. Can you explain the lag in the company's reaction?**

There was no lag. As noted above, Prolexic was retained as the wave of attacks began to intensify. The size, scope and intensity of the attacks were, to our knowledge, unprecedented. The denial-of-service attacks targeted multiple Sony Corporation companies and continued for days, but they only resulted in relatively brief outages of Sony Corporation company sites, and they never, in and of themselves, involved an actual or threatened intrusion into SNEA's network. The PlayStation Network was taken off line by SNEA executives because of the intrusion, not because of the denial-of-service attacks.

15.   **The security breaches at Sony have highlighted that in data security an ounce of prevention is worth a pound of cure. In this context, the first step when it comes to prevention is risk assessment. Before a company can determine how to allocate its resources, it must accurately identify high-risk areas. A company with consumer data must weigh two factors: (1) what information on its network is the most appealing for theft, and (2) what way to access its network is most vulnerable to attack.**

a.   **Had Sony previously prepared for the possibility that an attack like the one in April could occur?**

The denial-of-service attacks that occurred in April were, to our knowledge, unprecedented. The denial-of-service attacks were designed to force an end to legitimate legal action being pursued in Federal Court. Separately, as to the intrusion attack, SNEA understood that all networks are subject to hacker attack and built the robust information security system that protected its network to prevent such attempts. Unfortunately, that system was not successful in preventing this particular attack.

Letter to Honorable Mary Bono Mack &
Honorable G. K. Butterfield
July 21, 2011
Page 11 of 16

    b.   **How had Sony assessed the amount of risk that such an attack posed to the company?**

As noted, we did not anticipate the risk that bringing litigation would result in such a large scale sophisticated attack by anonymous hackers. Separately, and again, as to the intrusion attack, SNEA of course understood that hackers might attempt to penetrate its network and, aware of the potential risk to customer information and business goodwill, SNEA had built a robust security system in an effort to prevent such attempts. SNEA's procedure was to encrypt payment card data, and CVV2 codes were not collected or stored. Customer information was stored behind firewalls.

    c.   **Many companies undertake penetration testing of their systems on an annual basis. How, and how often, does Sony undertake penetration testing for its different networks?**

The testing of SNEA's systems includes both vulnerability scanning and penetration testing. Some of SNEA's systems were scanned as often as monthly, and comprehensive penetration testing had been performed in 2010. SNEA was in the process of moving its network into a new facility. Penetration testing was already in process for that facility at the time of the attack, which occurred shortly before the planned move.

    d.   **What other tools does the company have to ensure it has a proactive information security regime? For example, do your networks undergo regular third-party audits?**

SNEA's information security regime, including the manner in which its current data center was built, is guided by the above-referenced Sony Corporation policies and by applicable industry standards and best practices. A third-party assessment program for this facility is currently in progress. In addition, SNEA will continue to pursue ongoing education and research to ensure ongoing maintenance of evolving standards and practices and current knowledge of ever-evolving security threats so that, where appropriate, it can make corresponding adjustments to the security controls it has in place.

    e.   **What does Sony do to work with others in your industry and share information regarding data security, so that you can keep current regarding possible threats and assess them accurately?**

SNEA's security team monitors industry and other sites that disclose vulnerabilities, works closely with vendors of network infrastructure, participates regularly in prominent security-related conferences, and communicates and shares information with the various security officers of the many Sony Corporation companies.

Letter to Honorable Mary Bono Mack &
Honorable G. K. Butterfield
July 21, 2011
Page 12 of 16

      f.   **Given that Sony's networks have been repeatedly breached, it seems fair to say there was a failure of risk management. In light of these attacks, how have you changed your risk assessment approaches?**

No, it is not fair to say that there has been a failure of risk management. There was a breach of security systems, but this particular breach resulted from an attack by a hacker of uncommon ability. As the federal government itself has made clear, there is no such thing as perfect security. In light of these attacks, however, SNEA has become increasingly vigilant in its approach to data security attacks.

      g.   **Hackers continue to threaten Sony and many other companies. Do you believe you are prepared for the ongoing threat of attacks against Sony?**

We have enhanced the security already in place prior to the breach. In the aftermath of the original denial-of-service attacks against Sony Corporation company servers, hackers turned to other Sony Corporation companies and sites. The knowledge and available tools that SNEA acquired through the initial attacks are being shared among Sony Corporation companies. SNEA has enhanced the security already in place prior to the breach and believes that the safeguards it has in place are appropriate for addressing risks relating to possible future attacks against SNEA.

16.   **The news of the last several months indicates that successful, sophisticated cyber-attacks are on the rise. Since the beginning of 2011, major attacks have occurred against not just Sony and Epsilon, but also against security firm RSA and government contactor Lockheed Martin. Each one of these firms takes quite serious precautions against cyber-attacks, yet they experience breaches all the same. It is more important than ever that both the government and private corporations emphasize data security.**

      a.   **Have budgets for IT security at Sony kept pace as a percentage of operating costs over the last five years?**

Our network business has grown markedly in the last few years and security has been an increasing element of the operating budgets.

      b.   **Do you believe that your industry's IT professionals have the technical skills to keep pace with hackers and proactively protect your network?**

Yes, but it is worth noting that the hackers are also highly skilled. Security is an on-going concern that must always be addressed proactively.

      c.   **What changes do you believe need to be made in order for IT professionals to better understand the threats of the day—rather than those present at the time they were trained—as well as new methods to defend against attacks that occur?**

IT professionals need information about immediate threats and access to timely information of vulnerabilities. IT professionals need a forum and means of exchange where these threats can be shared and addressed. The difficulty is the risk in sharing information. As information is shared it also becomes available to the hacking community. Better cooperation between industry and government to encourage security is a first step. Better policing and monitoring of hackers by the government to discourage and prevent orchestrated criminal attacks would be helpful.

17.   **According to published reports, divisions of Sony have now been attacked on several occasions by the hacker group Lulz Security. One of these attacks was revealed during or close to the same time that you were testifying before the Committee on June 2, 2011. Lulz Security had previously launched a successful attack on PBS and had issued numerous Twitter messages before the Committee hearing indicating that it was in the process of transferring out internal Sony data. Yet the group still managed to allegedly access more than one million records and publicly post information from an estimated 37,500 Sony pictures web accounts. The next week, on June 6th, 2011 it was reported that the group had attacked Sony again, having released source code from the Sony Computer Entertainment Development Network as well as internal network maps of Sony BMG.**

a.   **When did you first learn that the network infrastructure of Sony Pictures Entertainment had been attacked by Lulz Security?**

SNEA learned of the attack on the sonypictures.com website when it was announced by Lulz Security on the day of the hearing.

b.   **If you learned about this attack prior to or during the hearing, why did you not divulge news of this attack to the Committee?**

I was unaware of the attack on the sonypictures.com website at the time of the hearing.

c.   **Do you know if Sony Pictures Entertainment had anticipated an attack by Lulz Security or any other similar group? Do you know what, if any steps, Sony Pictures Entertainment took to combat the attack and prevent unauthorized access to its user accounts?**

I am informed by Sony Pictures Entertainment that Sony Pictures Entertainment confirmed that sonypictures.com had been the target of an attack when Lulz Security publicly posted Sony Pictures Entertainment information on June 2, 2011. In conjunction with its announcement of the breach on June 3, 2011, Sony Pictures Entertainment stated that it had "taken action to protect against further intrusion" and had "contacted the U.S. Federal Bureau of Investigation and [was] working with them to assist in the identification and apprehension of those responsible for this crime."

d.   **Do you know if Sony Pictures Entertainment first received confirmation that the Lulz Security attack against Sony Pictures was successful at the same time the general**

Letter to Honorable Mary Bono Mack &
Honorable G. K. Butterfield
July 21, 2011
Page 14 of 16

public did—i.e., when news outlets discovered that the Lulz Security had indeed publicly posted the user account information it had obtained from the Sony Pictures network? If not, when did it receive this confirmation?

See above.

e.   Do you know how Sony Corporation and its major subsidiaries plan to retain customers' trust following these sustained and successful attacks, one of which seems to have occurred as one of its companies was testifying before Congress?

SNEA has worked hard to explain to its customers what it can about the attack, without disclosing information which would make itself or other companies more vulnerable to future attacks. SNEA has offered identity theft protection insurance as part of its Welcome Back package and has increased its security efforts. SNEA's customers have responded by overwhelmingly returning to SNEA's network. Also, as noted, in conjunction with its announcement of the breach on June 3, 2011, Sony Pictures Entertainment stated that it had "taken action to protect against further intrusion." SPE has also offered identity theft protection insurance to those users whose information may have been taken.

The Honorable John D. Dingell:

1.   Do you believe current industry efforts with respect to ensuring data security are sufficient?

SNEA believes that the industry is taking meaningful and intensive efforts to protect customers' data but no single company can sufficiently protect against outside criminal intrusions without a better coalition between the industry, government and law enforcement.

2.   Do you believe the Congress should pass comprehensive data security legislation?

Yes, because of the reach of the internet, uniform standards for giving customers notice of a breach and guidelines on how and when to inform customers of a breach would be beneficial for companies doing business online.

3.   Comprehensive data security requirements do not exist in the United States. Rather, there exists a patchwork of federal and state laws and regulations that impose varying requirements on entities. Should federal data security requirements supersede state requirements? Further, should state attorneys-general be allowed to enforce federal data security requirements?

Standard data security requirements could be helpful as long as the legislation did not attempt to set specific technical requirements. Legislation setting technical standards will inevitably become minimum standards as legislation, and even rulemaking will not be able to keep up with technological advances and ability of hackers to outpace the

Letter to Honorable Mary Bono Mack &
Honorable G. K. Butterfield
July 21, 2011
Page 15 of 16

legislation or rulemaking. Federal data security requirements should supersede state requirements to ensure uniformity. Whether or not state attorneys general should be allowed to enforce federal data security requirements would depend on the scope of the legislation. At this time, it is premature to make a recommendation.

4.   Do you believe federal data security legislation should include the flexibility for the Federal Trade Commission to update requirements in order to keep pace with the advancements in threats to data security?

Any federal legislation related to data security will have to anticipate that the technological landscape will change at a pace that legislation or regulatory agencies will have difficulty keeping pace with. If the purpose of the legislation is to set standards or requirements that industries must follow, then it seems unlikely that any agency would be able to keep pace with the advancements in potential threats to data security.

5.   Do you believe the FTC's cumbersome Magnusson-Moss rulemaking procedures would stifle the Commission's ability to write rules that keep pace with technological advancements in threats to data security? If so, do you believe the FTC should be allowed to write data security regulations according to the Administrative Procedure Act, which—while still thorough—is more expeditious process than Magnusson-Moss?

SNEA believes that any attempt to write rules that seek to keep pace with technological advancements in threats to data security will fail if the FTC, or any other agency, attempts to write regulations that set fixed technical standards or set specific technical requirements. The technology moves too fast in this area, and the threats come from an enemy that is capable of assimilating new technology very quickly.

6.   Further, I ask that both witnesses comment for the record on the reasonableness, appropriateness, and practicality of requiring in law that entities which hold personal data provide customers with some form of insurance to mitigate potential damages caused to them by data breaches.

Any legislation that would require companies to provide customers with some form of insurance to mitigate potential damages caused to them by data breaches would have to be carefully crafted to balance the actual harm to the customer, given the type of information at issue, with the burden on commerce that could result from the imposition of an insurance requirement. Balancing of that sort would need to take into account, for example, the potentially vastly different costs and effects of a requirement that insurance coverage be offered to those consumers that may have been potentially affected from a breach that has been in fact identified versus a requirement to secure automatic insurance coverage for consumers generally prior to any breach having occurred. Financial data, social security numbers, and medical information obviously have a greater potential for harm or mischief if the data is breached, than simple e-mail, or address information, which is more akin to information contained in the traditional white pages. Much basic information about individuals is widely available online, and companies should not be

Letter to Honorable Mary Bono Mack &
Honorable G. K. Butterfield
July 21, 2011
Page 16 of 16

penalized for the loss of data that is not confidential or private. One of the great values of the internet is that it allows small companies to market and distribute products and information on a scale that could only be done by companies many times their size just a few years ago. While businesses should not be allowed to trade in important private personal data or financial information without adequate protection and customers' approval, another important goal of any legislation should be not to quash the ability of small businesses to use the internet to compete against much larger companies by burdening them with costs that really do not advance or improve privacy online.

7.   I note that Sony is presently providing customers affected by its data breach with a one year identity theft insurance policy worth $ 1 million. I would ask that Sony submit for the record the cost to Sony and/or consumers of providing such insurance policies, as well as how many such policies are so far in effect.

SNEA has offered the insurance to all of its customers who had active accounts as of April 20, 2011. To date approximately 230,000 persons have signed up for the insurance. Contractual provisions constrain SNEA from providing cost information. SNEA has extended the offering for an additional month and contacted customers directly to insure that customers who were offered the insurance have an opportunity to secure the protection if they feel it is warranted.

<u>The Honorable Mary Bono Mack</u>:

Please provide an update to your prior responses from the committee. In particular, please provide details on subsequent breaches and any significant information that has come to light since your prior response.

No significant information has come to light regarding the breach of SNEA's network since our response dated May 26, 2011. At or around the time of the first hearing, there were several news reports that other Sony Corporation companies had been breached and large amounts of personal information may have been taken. Investigation into those breaches has determined that the number of affected persons is much smaller than originally claimed. There have been no successful breaches of SNEA's network since the hearing.

On behalf of SNEA, I hope that in answering these questions we have been helpful to the Committee.

Very truly yours,

Tim Schaaff
President
Sony Network Entertainment America Inc.